WHAT OTHERS ARE SAYING ABOUT MADELAINE COHEN

"I have known Madelaine for several years and have witnessed her unique panache and passion for business, entrepreneurialism and marketing and would have no hesitation in recommending her to any business, individual or organisation looking to engage Madelaine.

Madelaine has a breadth of experience including start-ups, successful businesses and consultancy and her experience coupled with her infectious drive and determination, as well as knowledge enable her to coach and empower others with little effort.

When Madelaine gets involved in a new project, she is 150% committed and just makes it work and her latest venture proves just that. You will never regret your decision to engage or work with Madelaine, just do it."

Kylie Green
Managing Director - Activations, MKTG Australia at Dentsu Aegis Network

"Madelaine is a focused, highly organised, efficient business person. I have worked with her for 11 years and would highly recommend her business savvy in any business."

Megan Kassel
Sole Trader at GGM Accounting Services

The
Lateral-Thinking
ENTREPRENEUR

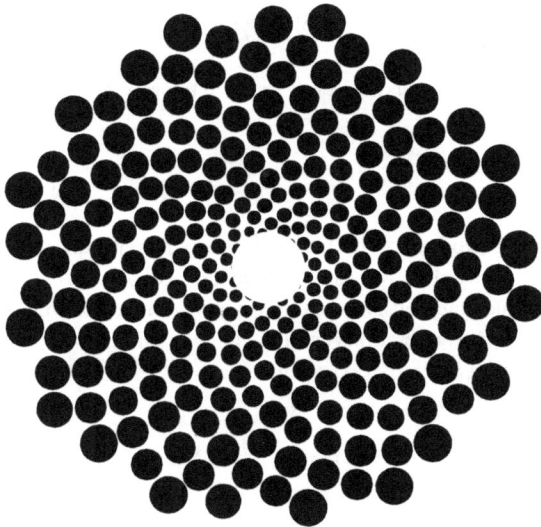

33 Principles For
Expansive Leadership

Madelaine Cohen

Premium Wellness
PUBLISHING

DISCLAIMER

The information contained within this book is strictly for educational purposes and is for general comment only. If you wish to apply ideas contained in this book, you are taking full responsibility for your actions. The author has made every effort to ensure the accuracy of the information within this book was correct at time of publication. The author does not assume and hereby disclaims any liability to any party for any loss, damage, or disruption caused by errors or omissions, whether such errors or omissions result from accident, negligence, or any other cause. It is recommended that the reader obtain their own independent advice.

Names and identifying details have been changed to protect the identity of individuals.

Cover Design and Pre-Press: Tash Lewin (Brand Your Book)

Edited by: Julie Lewin (Brand Your Book)

National Library of Australia

Cataloguing-in-Publication entry:

Cohen, Madelaine, 1971-

The Lateral-Thinking Entrepreneur: 33 Principles for Expansive Leadership

1st Edition

ISBN: 978-0-9953926-0-1

1. Entrepreneur 2. Leadership 3. Strategies 4. Career 5. Spiritual

Published by Premium Wellness Publishing

PO Box 1686, Bondi Junction NSW 1355 Australia

Email: madelaine@madelainecohen.com

Phone: + 61 2 9211 8153

DEDICATION

*To the amazing souls who have taught me,
mentored me and taken the high road with me
My gratitude is beyond words*

*To the amazing souls who I mentor and
who work in my businesses,
your willingness to be extraordinary
is awesome and my inspiration*

ACKNOWLEDGEMENTS

It has taken the best part of twelve years on the high road to write this book. When my first born child arrived in 2004 I realised that I had something worth sharing to inspire and connect. February 2004 was the turning point in a heartbreaking rollercoaster ride of five years of IVF treatment, a devastating miscarriage and finally the arrival of a much wanted child that made me realise the resources within me that had enabled me to accomplish so much and to set a new standard for myself and others. It was going within and listening to my own soul that enabled me to become a mother. I learnt that my outward expression was a factor of my internal existence and I had discovered the power of this in manifesting both positive and negative outcomes. The night before I gave birth, I signed a deal with my colleague Catherine Mair and the Melbourne Organising Committee for the 2006 Commonwealth Games to deliver their multi-million dollar consumer products marketing and retail programs. I knew that I could take the high road and live within a system of excellence to be everything and do anything. Most of all I knew I was to be of service. I am forever grateful for the tenacity and insights of my journey to motherhood.

The process of bringing my gorgeous son Mac into the world made me contemplate the resources and strategies I use every day. I sought even more learning and attended almost every seminar Anthony Robbins has ever produced travelling the world seeking to understand. I completed Harry Palmer's Avatar Courses, became certified in Reiki II with Ghata Engels, tuned into my intuitive abilities with Sylvie Orville Blue, became a certified Neuro-Linguistic Programming Master Practitioner and Trainer and a Master Practitioner and Trainer of Matrix Therapeutic

Coaching with Lauren Jobson and Pip McKay and the pieces of my learning started to accelerate.

My precious daughter Indiana was born in 2007 and her free spirit and "can do" attitude to life is like watching the best movie ever. When my IVF specialists told me this was my last chance I asked for a blessing from the universe. Indiana is that blessing.

I also want to acknowledge my former husband Dr Michael Cohen, Chiropractor for his incredible technical skills as a Chiropractor. Michael inspired me to develop an outstanding business model to enable health-care practitioners to thrive in practice and his passion for delivering the best in Chiropractic care is remarkable.

In 2009, my father Theo died very suddenly and in losing him I received an incredible gift. Within days of his passing I was given evidence of his eternal presence. I asked for the signs and time again they were revealed like magic. Six weeks after he died his only sister had a debilitating stroke. In palliative care at Prince of Wales Hospital in Randwick she was mo-tionless and unable to speak. I visited her each day for 11 days. On the eleventh day, a Friday, I had seen her in the morning and by mid-afternoon I knew I had to go back to the hospital. I quickly organised my young children, dropped them off to their grandmother and went back to be at my aunt's side. Her breathing was laboured. I sang some Jewish prayers to her and I felt this incredible presence of angelic beings enter her room. I knew it was time for her to go and so I said to her, "There are beautiful angels here ready to take you and if you are ready to go, climb onto their wings. May God bless you and keep you always and may your memory be eternal." And with this she left her body. To this day I believe my father helped me to be by my aunt's side as she took her last breath. In this moment, I knew that my connection to source was a truth and I want to acknowledge him and my aunty Peppi for this gift.

In 2012, my dear friend and healer Louise Kelly suggested I connect with Julie Lewin. I refused the call. Then one Sunday in early 2013 I decided to email Julie to have a chat about her work. I felt as though I had met a kindred soul and someone who would ultimately be an incredible mentor for me. In June 2013, I spent a week with Julie on an intensive deep dive retreat and my world transformed in the most incredible way. I found my purpose. Since 2013, I have worked with Julie. We have laughed and we have loved. Travelled to Uluru together for sacred connection work with Belinda Pate-MacDonald and in 2015 I travelled to Sedona in the USA to attend one of Julie's international retreats. It was amazing. I am so grateful to have Julie in my life and for her to be the editor of my books.

My life today is full of love and connection thanks to my partner Michael Jeffreys. A huge thank you.

CONTENTS

Foreword

Preface

Introduction

1. Seek to Understand..5

2. Goals are only scored in team sport..............................9

3. Outsource...15

4. Gratitude..21

5. Freedom..27

6. Drama..33

7. Mistakes..41

8. World Within the World...47

9. Self-Control..55

10. Physiology...61

11. Ideas...67

12. Different...75

13. Cylinder...79

14. Empathy...85

15. Limitations..91

16. Clarity..95

17. Separating heart from head...101

18. A quantum leap at the centre of your universe...........107

19. Looking for 2%...113

20. Pro-bono. Who are you kidding?.........................117

21. Eating an Elephant...121

22. Being followed by idiots..125

23. Doing indispensable when you seek appreciation.......................131

24. Say Goodbye to procrastination...........................137

25. Money or Money & Mentor?..................................143

26. The currency for your expertise is money...........147

27. Attitude..151

28. Embracing Change..157

29 Activity to Create a Compelling Future...............161

30. Seizing the opportunity...167

31. Who do you need to be?..173

32. Responsibility..177

33. Success through others..181

Transform your success even more.............................185

About the author..189

FOREWORD

The skill set for Leadership is forever evolving. If you have tertiary qualified in the past 3 years or the past 20 years, the fundamentals of corporate management don't alter a great deal.

I have been a Truck Driver, Commercial Pilot, Business owner, Bank Manager and latterly I am revisiting leadership and management in Retail Banking once again.

The passion and purpose you discover for yourself as a leader I believe is very personal and there is no real right way but plenty of Mistakes can be made I can attest to the latter ! Personally I found great peace and encouragement reading your lesson on this - I'm urging all leaders to take particular note here, it could just be that element that tinkers on success or not quite so successful.

It takes extraordinary courage to continue to learn and develop your leadership skills, I search and read and am still tertiary studying now...

What I found in reading this book is the most profound dimensional shift in leadership and management in easy to learn format that I have read in the past 5 years.

This book will test you, it is not a book to skim through, it is a philosophy built on sensible common sense approach that will bring immediate Balance into your Emotional, Physical, Mental, Spiritual and Financial world. It is a must have in 2016 in all leadership roles.

It will challenge your beliefs, set new ones in place and refocus you in the most unusual and interesting way I have experienced yet.

We are working with people and people are changing, - they don't change yearly! Just like you don't! Are we listening? Are we being Congruent? Are these things really important? What are behaviours? How do your actions precede you daily? If you thought that Management and Leadership was a title having letters after your name...let me leave you with this...

I will never look at the holistic "Nanu Nanu" the same...who would have thought 25 years later that I would resonate with such a simple TV show! – In Retail Banking the leadership spectrum is easy to follow and a must for coping with behaviours that are unexpected nor welcomed.. to distance yourself and to Lead through this is probably the biggest take away strategy that has enhanced my own skills in the past 4 weeks.

Madelaine eludes to movies and watching the scenes play out...so are we actually the main actor in our own movie or are we the props? Which role is your destiny?

Madelaine Cohen – Thank you for sharing your insights in a timely well thought out book, I can't wait to have this one on my library shelf along with more to come. Having kept it simple you have added some dimensional challenging shifts that I still am working through but isn't it great to be challenged and to learn to understand...?

The Lateral –thinking Entrepreneur – 33 Principles of expansive leadership, will bring together Personality profiling at the most basic and useful of techniques – Your Leadership and Management skills can only be enhanced here. – It is without doubt the "Point of Difference"

Lance Harding
Bank Manager
Bank of Queensland

PREFACE

Do you realise what you are truly capable of? You are capable of amazing things. And when you connect the thoughts in your head, with the power of observation and then create a step-by-step plan to bring your intuition and lateral-thinking into the world you live in, the things you will accomplish are remarkable.

In this book, I am going to show you how the messages and processes in your head are the secret to lateral-thinking success. This is the simplicity and power of living in two worlds. The world within your being and the world that is tangible and requires you to engineer the right circumstances for you to shine and live the life of your destiny dreams.

This book will not change your life unless you choose for your life to change. The high road is never easy and yet it is infinitely more rewarding than living a life of quiet desperation. This book has been written to share with you the thinking processes that have enabled me to be a successful entrepreneur, mentor and business owner for 25 years.

My gift to you is this: have courage and be inspiring. Do whatever it takes to live in a place of service to yourself and others. Choose to be a leader. Every new movement starts with a leader and your first follower. I hope you are able to connect with the magnificent world within every cell of the person that is you and then take your unique gift to the world as a change-maker to create a greater good for yourself, your community and your world.

With love & gratitude,

Madelaine Cohen

Entrepreneur / Business Mentor / Author

INTRODUCTION

It's funny and almost embarrassing that at the age of twenty-one I decided to "retire" from employment and begin a career as a business leader. I can hear the laughter because today we'd refer to a young woman who does this as having no idea and the assumption would be that she would never succeed. You have the picture.

Fast forward twenty five years and I am here to share my story with you.

At the age of twenty-one, I became an entrepreneur and business leader by choice. I decided that age would be no barrier, and that my height would never deter me. My journey became a learning experience and every year I have studied something new, taken courses and opened my knowledge base. I will continue to do this for the rest of my life.

I believe that everyone has unlimited potential to manifest whatever they want in their life and that shrinking so other people feel secure is a poor way to be enlightened. My existence is about communication, human to human communication that creates results for myself and others and opens pathways to leadership and success.

In this book you will find the principles I use in my business and leadership every day. They are easy to do and easy not to do steps that create what I call the "slipstream of success". This slipstream is a place of accelerated happiness that lies between the drama of the ordinary world and the cop out of living in la la land. I call it living an extraordinary life in an ordinary world.

Communication skills and thought processes are an important part of what I share. I have always believed you can be the most skilled person in the world in your field and yet if you are challenged by mastering communication with others, your internal dialogue and the way you interpret external events, your success in business, leadership or career will be mediocre at best.

I finished my high school education at Kambala in Sydney. The Year 12 Higher School Certificate is my last formally completed education. I have committed myself to a lifetime of learning and education through reading, courses and personal development on a continual basis.

My early career was in retail management until I started my own business as a consultant. I pulled together a team of experts and for 17 years consulted to the marketing departments of some of the largest sporting events in the world. My clients included organising committees for the Olympic Games, Commonwealth Games and Asian Games where my team would deliver multi-million dollar licensed merchandise, retail and consumer products marketing projects. In this time, I gained an interest in consumer behaviour, communication and healthcare. I became involved as the co-owner of a large Chiropractic business in Sydney and found myself mentoring Drs on communication, client retention and marketing. This was so successful that I decided to buy the business from my former partner.

Today, I mentor business people, executives, healthcare professionals and managers in the areas of communication, strategy, planning, business and financial success.

In this book, you will learn the steps to unpacking strategies for communication success in a whole new dimension in leadership, client communication, delegation and in business.

CHAPTER 1:
SEEK TO UNDERSTAND

"Everything that irritates us about others can lead us to an understanding of ourselves." ~ C.G. Jung

The very first principle in business and leadership I use every day comes from a high level of behavioural flexibility. The word flexibility means the quality of bending without breaking.

There is no one else in the world just like you and at the same time there are tribes of people who are just like you. I am a twin. At my birth, my mother had no idea she was having two babies. No sooner had I arrived when an apparent flurry of activity was immediately set into motion. The hospital staff could see another baby making her way into the world. As a child, I knew my sister and I were not the same person, and yet we were treated as one. We were nameless being referred to as the twins. This was normal and never a concern for me.

As an adult, I became accustomed to answering to my sister's name. I live in Sydney, Australia and yet, one day I was half a world away in London and I could hear a voice calling my sister's name from across the street. It was one of her work colleagues also travelling and she was convinced I was my sister.

My mother was told at my birth that my sister and I were non-identical twins and yet we felt otherwise. Looking at photos of each other growing up and even as adults we could not tell the difference and often could not work out who was who in the photos. Imagine looking at a photo of yourself and being unable to determine if it's actually you that you are looking at?

At the age of thirty, instead of a birthday gift we opted for a DNA test and sat together one night scraping the insides of our mouths with sterile pipe cleaner sticks as we prepared to send our cells off to a laboratory to determine whether we were in fact identical twins. When the results arrived I was overseas and so my sister waited until I was back in the country before we opened the envelopes together. The result was astounding our DNA is 99.98% identical. In non-identical twins DNA is about 50% the same.

I am constantly asked what it's like to be a twin. In return I ask, "what is it like not being a twin?" I cannot answer the twin question. The truth is I have no idea because I have nothing to compare it to.

The experience of being a twin has helped me appreciate the nuances of being, at many times, nameless as a human being. I was instead the label "twin". When people believe you are exactly the same as another human being the perspective on human interaction that validates your identity becomes an interesting and complex puzzle.

To understand means to interpret or view something in a particular way. Behaviour means the way in which someone acts or conducts themselves.

What is involved in understanding behaviour is profound. Life experiences, beliefs, values, family of origin, geography, religion, education, state of health all impact how an individual views the world. An opinion and a belief is neither right nor wrong, it "just is" based on the person who has formed it.

It is important to have an expansive view of understanding when it comes to other people. This helps you to live in a place of calm self-assurance. You can be in the place where you don't need to take anything personally and where you have ultimate control of your own responses. Being open to accepting people exactly as they are is liberating in leadership. This does not mean you stay in process with people who you dislike or who are not good for you. It means having the level of understanding to be able to move away or stay, choose carefully and always be in a place of being grounded in your leadership.

Here are some ideas on gaining a greater depth of understanding in human behaviours:

- People are not what they do. Separate people from their actions.

- To change someone, change your own actions.

- The choices people make are their own responsibility.

- The choices you make are your own responsibility.

- When you seek to understand, you ask questions and listen for the response.

- The meaning you elicit from a response will always be based on your life experiences and values.

- How would you act in the event that you had the viewpoint of seeing the truth without judgment. The highest form of seeking to understand is removing all judgement in the labels right and wrong.

- The only thing you need to be aware of in interactions with others is the meaning you give to the experience.

- To allow an individual the freedom to experience their own life journey and simply provide your inspiration - whether it is adopted or not - is one of the greatest leadership actions you may ever take.

Being a twin has been an enormous benefit in my life and in leadership. It has helped me seek to understand at a depth I doubt I could have experienced as a singleton. My sister and I are very individual and yet visually we are not easy to separate. Even we have problems working out who is who. Looking in her eyes is sometimes like looking into a mirror. And yet it isn't real. There is a new depth of human observation that evolves when you have someone who is just like you walking around in the world and yet you are your own individual person.

So much human upset in leadership comes from the illusion of control. When you seek to understand another human being there is no control. The only feedback you receive is a consequence of your own behaviours and your own contributions to the world.

CHAPTER 2:
GOALS ARE ONLY SCORED IN TEAM SPORT

"If you want to live a happy life, tie it to a goal, not to people or things." ~ Albert Einstein

When I first started in business at age 21, I had lots of goals. I'd read a lot about the pros and cons of either bleating your goals to the world or keeping them private and close to your chest. Most of the time, it felt better to keep my goals and dreams to myself because I really thought I would be talked out of them by well-meaning friends and family. This was perhaps wise as I knew that the decisions I'd already made to go into my own business were misaligned with what they believed to be possible.

It wasn't until years later that I learnt the honest truth about goals and this happened when I was consulting to the Marketing Department of the Sydney Olympic Games Organising Committee. In an organisation that had literally thousands of staff, I was in sports marketing as an outsider on the inside (which is how I feel as a consultant in big companies). I was sitting in a meeting one day where collaborative logistics across departments, stakeholders, nations and the International Olympic Committee were being discussed in the hope of bringing together a combined outcome otherwise known in my mind as scoring a goal. In this moment, it dawned on me that in sport goals are only scored when a team is involved. I was literally and unashamedly looking out the window onto the old brewery across Broadway trying to think of any individual sport that involved scoring a goal. And I couldn't think of one!

I am not all that good at, nor absolutely passionate about sport. So 17 years in sports marketing was an incredible learning curve for me. When it comes to sport, spin class is about as much as I can deal with. It used to be a joke amongst colleagues at the Olympic and Commonwealth Games Organising Committee's that I was not in the industry for the chance to see incredible events. My time in sports marketing did teach me many great things, and one of these is my understanding of goals and how they are achieved.

Modelling the attributes of successful sports teams scoring goals transformed how I deal with my business goals.

This brings me to the first step of goal scoring; going toward it!

You don't normally see someone scoring a goal by running away from it. In sport, it's generally the theme that when you want to score a goal, you need to go toward it. So when you set a goal the next step is to take actions, no matter how small, to go toward it. What this taught me is that when you set a goal in business, you need to take steps toward it like the player on the field. This is by far the most critical step in achieving your goals. So I started to really tune into this in business and I suggest you do it, too. When a player is moving toward a goal in sport they are predatory, there's no lying around in the grass looking at the clouds after deciding to go for a goal. There's no passive fear involved. There are opposing players to negotiate, paths of least resistance to find, other people who are on your team to help the journey and a goal to be scored.

The second step of goal scoring is to observe your competition.

In business the opposition are your competition and you need to be aware of what they are doing. I am a realist and in business I believe that being aware of competition in your peripheral vision is important. Everyone has great ideas and there is plenty of space for organisations in the same markets and industry to thrive and succeed. Learn from what's going on around you. Be present to the positions of your competition. Teams in sport know that their opposition plays a role in their scoring ability. In business this is the same.

The third step of goal scoring is to choose your best team.

As a business owner you're the captain, the CEO, the person who decides who needs to be on the team. Once you've selected the best people, you need to work with them. In business, your team are your trusted supporters, your advisers, accountant, business mentor, staff (if you have them), contractors and your suppliers of goods and services that you need to achieve your goal. In team sport it's a fluke when a player singlehandedly scores a goal. Mostly a goal is achieved by using the resources of other players either through their assistance with passing, their methods for obstructing players who want to stop the goal being scored or their advice as they support and call out to you on your journey to scoring. The captain leads the strategy and a good captain gets involved in the game at the grassroots level.

For every goal you want to achieve in business you need to work out who your players are. In my businesses when I've had goals to achieve I create a group of trusted advisors around me. For many years now this has been a monthly phone meeting with my accountant, financial advisor, a business mentor and myself on the line. We collaborate and discuss progress and how I am tracking with my business and goals. It doesn't need to be as sophisticated as this, it could be that you have a few trusted friends who are willing to be your sounding board and help you with ideas to keep you moving toward your goal and who can give you honest and caring critique on your actions. Then I choose the best suppliers and service providers for what I need. This means quality product or service, on time delivery and exceptional performance. All of these attributes are important in business. That's why you are in control of choosing the best team.

The fourth step of goal scoring is to know your field and layout.

The best teams in sport know their entire field and when to play in each section. In business, this is your market and you need to know your entire field. Imagine or if you cannot imagine remember what a football field looks like. It's a rectangle with various lines and a goal at either end. You have to protect your goal, which to me is your market share, your brand and your intellectual property at one end and you have your goal-keeper doing this job. Then you need to cover your entire field or market to score your goal at the other end of the field. When you imagine your market like a football field, it gives you an expansive view and the scope to make strategic decisions about how to move across your entire market and maximise every opportunity.

I use the S.M.A.R.T. acronym to plan a goal. In this acronym "s" refers to specific and simple. The "m" refers to measurable and meaningful to you. The "a" refers to achievable, and "r" refers to realistic and responsible. The "t" refers to timed and toward what you want. This way I can create a goal on a piece of paper and make sure that it is congruent with who I am as well as ecological and for the benefit and good of others too.

Sport is not my thing, and goal setting is. Sport has taught me some fundamental principles that can be used to help achieve a goal even faster. The world of sports marketing was an intriguing introduction to the differences between "team sport" and "individual sport" athlete achievement at an elite level. In reference to achieving goals, key secrets can be found in the reality of what it takes to score goals in sport. You can use this parallel to model your own actions around achieving goals. Setting goals is something I prefer to do on my own, and many entrepreneurs and business owners do the same due to their desire to be individual and to lead. What I found though is that if I kept my goals a secret my ability to achieve them was slower than I had hoped. The breakthrough came when I applied the model of scoring goals in team sport and mirrored the elite strategies used by the best teams in the Olympic and Common-wealth Games team sport events. Consequently, my approach became one of opening my goals to the assistance of others and it never being about them boosting or deflating my self-confidence. I sought the in-volvement of others based on clear strategic actions and tasks that were a direct result of using the tactics and methods of great teams. This approach motivates everyone around you to follow a plan with you and help you achieve your goals even faster and with a great deal of momentum.

CHAPTER 3:
OUTSOURCE

"Outsourcing is inevitable, and I don't think it's necessarily treating people like things." ~ Stephen Covey

In leadership, the pace of life is not easy. I frequently hear that high-functioning professionals and people in leadership roles are suffering from symptoms of adrenal fatigue at increased rates. In this chapter, I show you how to free up hours of your time every week and at the same time, establish space in your mind for the creative leadership thinking that you need to live your full potential.

When my first born child was very young he liked to be rocked to sleep. He was just a couple of months old and I decided to adhere to the community nurse's instructions and go to the local mother's group to meet other mothers. As an older mother, who worked right up until the night before having said child (in fact at 8pm on the day before his birth, I signed a highly lucrative, three-year contract for an international event), I was somewhat isolated from other mothers and did not have the heart to tell the community nurse that my bottle-fed son was already accompanying me to business meetings.

Already feeling out of place with bottle in hand, the discussion about how long it took to put children to bed clinched it. One mother at the group mentioned that she patted her now toddler daughter's bottom for an hour every night to help her settle. The child was three years old. This lady was now the mother of a newborn who needed to be held and jiggled at bedtime for at least 30 minutes and sometimes longer. The analytical businesswoman in me started calculating! One hour, 365 days a year, that's 365 hours. Then, second child, 30 minutes a night. Okay, so let's assume a normal person has 8 hours sleep per night, divide that by normal waking hours in a day of 16. Right, that means that this mother is going to spend a full 34 days, more than one whole month of equivalent daytime hours, for the whole year, patting and jiggling children to sleep! I could hardly cope with the thought.

This was my first and last time at a mother's group and that night I took my son home and started searching the internet for books on how to teach babies to self-settle. I could not buy one fast enough as I was about to lose a whole month of my life if I did not teach him how to sleep by himself. From that night onwards, I taught him and within a few weeks he was happily self-settling and I was relieved to have gained my life back, well sort of. This experience made me think about how busy we are with activities that we can outsource. One thing that came straight to mind was making it the child's responsibility to go to sleep.

I started thinking, how could I outsource with little cost and maximum time benefit?

Outsourcing in a business sense means to contract work out. Businesses do this activity to save money and increase time efficiencies and outcomes. In leadership, I define outsourcing as any action that has a task or activity completed through another person, a self-invented efficiency, time leverage or with technology. Today, I have taken my refinement of outsourcing to a level that is so exciting the illusion of how much I achieve becomes a quandary for many people I deal with.

Between running several businesses, speaking engagements, board appointments, going to the gym seven days a week, being mum to my two children, cooking gourmet meals and enjoying my friendships, I can appreciate that it looks as though I must never sleep. I've even developed ways to outsource my troubles and stresses. The benefits of outsourcing are many, including increased personal time, the ability to lead and be focussed in a relaxed manner, quality time with my friends and most importantly for leadership, the time to plan and work at a high level of efficiency. This strategy removes many obstacles to health problems and overwhelm, stress and anxiety, hence, outsourcing my troubles.

According to an annual research study conducted by the Australian Institute of Psychology (2014), one in four adults suffers from stress. The highest reported incidence of stress is in the 26 to 35 year age category. The main causes of stress include family at 45 percent, health at 42 percent, work at 32 percent and relationships at 31 percent. With a results score of over 81,600,000, Google "not enough time stress".

The step-by-step methodology I have used to create time space is based on my theory of the benefits of outsourcing.

Step 1: Empower the people around you

I started this in all areas of my life by edifying the people around me in order to bring out the best in them. I can people-please as a leader, by commending great work and encouraging more of it. What this does is bring out the best in others, making them efficient and effective. This is a great skill in all areas of your life, from family and friends, to children and partners. Let other people know what they can do to help you and encourage them by being grateful.

Step 2: Do an audit of your time

For one typical week, write down how you spend every minute of your time. From travelling to meetings, work time to lunch, shopping to cooking, sleeping to dressing, going to the gym to social activities. Jot it all down. As you do this, mark with a green highlighter pen, everything that makes you feel energised and alive. Everything you feel neutral about, mark with a yellow highlighter pen. Everything you find that drains your energy, mark with an orange highlighter pen. At the end of the week, add up the time spent in green, then yellow and then orange.

How are you spending your time? Is it energising you, or draining you?

Step 3: Review your orange items first

What are the items that could be eliminated or outsourced at little material cost and with the outcome of increasing available time? Some ideas I used for this included buying groceries online, which saved 90 minutes per week. This equates to 78 hours a year, translating to almost five full waking-hour days!

Next, I visited the local stores that I shop at all the time, explaining that I am trying to save time, and I asked them if they would deliver to my home at no charge. They all agreed. Calling the green grocer, dry cleaner, fish shop, pharmacy and butcher with my order requirements while driving to work saved me about two hours a week, so another six and a half full waking-hour days saved.

Next, I worked out how many regular meetings could be conducted over Skype, instead of face to face, in order to save travel time going to and from meetings. Four regular, weekly client meetings qualified and the saved travel time was three hours a week, which translated to 156 hours a year or nine and three quarter days a year. The first year I started this project I was the full-time working mother of a newborn and I saved myself thirty full days of daylight. Without missing out on anything and at no extra cost!

Step 4: Create a Full Task List

Take your to-do lists, or if you are storing your tasks in your head, write down a full list of what's on your mind, as tasks. Next, divide the list into two. Place anything that is urgent on one side, and anything important, but not urgent, on the other. With the two lists side by side, look at tasks that could be grouped. For example, place things to do with home and family together, personal and well-being items can co-exist, as can work and business or events and one-off activities. Intuitively create four - six categories that you could group the tasks into. Now, with these categories in mind, investigate whether an entire category could be outsourced. If you could, how might that look in terms of cost-benefit and time-saving?

What if it's not easy for you to find ways to outsource and save time? You may want to consider whether you have any secondary gain related to always wanting to be super busy. How is this serving you? As a leader, do you feel that unless you are incredibly busy all the time you are not fulfilling the rules of mass consciousness in defining how you should be living your life?

It has now been eleven years since I started outsourcing and in more recent times, I have taken my outsourcing to a new level. Like many leaders, I have worries and concerns and sometimes my inner dialogue does not serve my highest ideals. So I've become really comfortable with outsourcing all the help I need to live in peace and harmony within my mind and my soul. I achieve this through contemplation, meditation, trusted friends and mentors and through connecting to my spirituality. This has, by far, been the most quantum shift in freeing my time. How much time do you spend worrying and strategising in your head?

I trust you have a vision of how your life may look with time freedom. If it feels right for you to give yourself the gift of time, embrace outsourcing in both practical ways and in the way you lead yourself with your internal dialogue.

CHAPTER 4:
GRATITUDE

"Do not spoil what you have by desiring what you have not; remember that what you now have was once among the things you only hoped for." ~ Epicurus

Gratitude is thankfulness for all that is. Appreciation on the other hand is standing in the light of truth and experiencing something as it is. Stop for a moment and tune into the thoughts that come up when you think about gratitude.

Do you have a feeling, are you perhaps hearing the word "gratitude", or do you have a vision or a scene in your mind?

Is gratitude uplifting you or is it draining you?

Does it feel like it would take a lot of effort to override reality and take on the task of "having gratitude"?

One day, I was at a health clinic waiting for my appointment and I picked up the clinic's newsletter. The headline article was about gratitude. It had thoughtfully been written about all the ways you can show gratitude. The ideas were many, including specific words and actions of gratitude. Ranking high on the list were smiling at people, speaking to and thanking people, and random acts of kindness.

As I read through the article, I noticed that my body started to feel tired and overwhelmed. A part of me wanted to remember all the actions, and then another part of me felt that to do all these "gratitude things" felt draining. It was literally draining my energy. I really wanted to unpack this feeling and find out why I felt this way. Then I had the most amazing moment, a moment in which I realised what gratitude really is.

Gratitude is defined as a quality of being thankful and a readiness to show appreciation for kindness. In this regard, it is something that you do. We are taught to exercise gratitude through acts.

As the leader you are, I want to turn this around for you. The word gratitude comes from the Latin word "gratia," meaning grace. When I think about the word "grace" I have a sense of something in flow. Grace, to me, means a smooth and elegant movement. What if gratitude involved less about **doing** and more about a state of **being**, a state that is smooth and elegant? What if this state was entirely expansive and set you apart in how you lead your life and how you show up as a leader to others?

My definition of gratitude is just that. It involves being in a smooth and elegant state of energetic co-creation, instead of a state of just "doing." Rest with that for a moment. Close your eyes and feel what it is like to just be in a state of gratitude, without having to make any effort or do anything?

Can you define gratitude as an emotional state within your body that is prefaced by a state of deep stillness, smooth elegance and balance and then just a feeling of heartfelt openness and space within you?

Gratitude, as it is best experienced in 21st Century leadership, is an assured state of expansive presence, where you dear leader, can simply be in the deepest, graceful stillness of you.

Living in this place enables your leadership approach to truly bring out the best in yourself and others, without any effort. It takes all of your authenticity to be in a place of deep and graceful stillness and this is calming and nurturing to your nervous system. This approach also helps to eliminate stress and pressure. Most importantly, it takes the "doing" effort out of your leadership approach, taking you out of a state of high alert and action.

In Hebrew, the expression for gratitude is *hakarat hatov* and the literal translation of this is "recognising the good." There's no effort required to simply recognise the good. The best way to do this is to be in a state of stillness and open-heartedness because you can hear a pin drop when the mind clutter is clear. How does this relate to effort and doing? It simply doesn't.

I have always been inspired by this quote from John F Kennedy who once said, "As we express our gratitude, we must never forget that the highest appreciation is not to utter words, but to live by them." I take this to mean living your authentic self. In 2010, Psychologists Emmons and Mishra studied the benefits of the emotional state of gratitude and its impact on wellbeing. They found that gratitude is a virtue that by nature must be deliberately cultivated, and the state of gratitude arises from a posture of openness with others. They also found gratitude to be foundational to wellbeing and mental health, citing scientific evidence of these benefits which resulted from studies in which patients with neuromuscular disease and hypersensitivity were found to have increased psychological wellbeing in the context of experiencing and being exposed to gratitude. They describe the highest experience of gratitude as coming from a stable mood, and that this was found to have long lasting benefits for consciousness.

How gratitude becomes a state of being instead of an act of doing requires some lateral-thinking around the very premise I find many leaders hold closely to their identity. The premise revolves around beliefs about the effort of leadership, the journey of heroism and the pinnacles of achievement associated with the worthiness of leadership. Often, leaders in business build their identity through the tireless and thankless task of effort beyond human limits. Is this why leadership is not so easy? To let go of the "doing" means to be completely authentic in the space of gratitude. As such, the spontaneity of living in a place of deep stillness and feeling heartfelt openness, becomes a way of life.

Have you ever had the experience of walking into a room where the energy feels uncomfortable? Sometimes you might refer to this as, "being able to cut the air with a knife." Have you also had the experience of being around someone whose energy radiates with so much happiness and love that you just want to smile? There's no coincidence that the energy signatures of these contexts show us that we are energetic beings who can connect to matter that we just cannot see. It is valuable to stop and appreciate here that the secret to gratitude I share with you gives you an experience of grace that will be felt by others. As a leader, there is literally nothing you need to say in order for people around you to know that you embody deep gratitude.

What follows is an easy exercise that allows you to bring more gratitude into your daily experience.

EXERCISE: Stand up and feel the ground beneath your feet. Find a place of stillness by taking three long, restful breaths and feel your shoulders sink down and move further away from your ears as you exhale. As you do this, visualise an imaginary ribbon, called a figure-of-eight ribbon, which goes from your solar plexus down to the ground in front of you, into the earth. This is the point where the figure of eight crosses over itself. It then goes out of the earth and into the space ahead of you. In that space might be nothing, an inanimate object like a piece of furniture, a person, a tree or plant. Allow the ribbon to go through whatever is there. From this point, it will return, through the earth, and back to you. Just as there is no end to the figure of eight, the energy exchange will continue to cycle. This ribbon, and how it flows ahead of you, is your ribbon of gratitude.

This exchange demonstrates the energy signature of gratitude, and it has a secret. The secret is that once you put it ahead of you every day, it continues to work without you needing to do a task or make an action-based effort. Why? It's because a figure of eight is also the infinity symbol. This is your being in gratitude. Just having this infinite exchange through the grounding of the Earth ahead of you allows you to be in gratitude in a manner that is felt by others, by your surroundings and even by inanimate objects; without you doing anything or having to say anything, unless it is completely spontaneous.

Sometimes the state of gratitude can confuse. The reason for this is that it has many dimensions. It can be experienced as a human behavioural characteristic, an emotion state and a mood. The most important aspect of staying in the highest state of gratitude depends on your mood. And this is because you are in charge of your mood and can adapt it consciously. If you are able to maintain your frame of mind or mood in a state of gratitude, you will experience the benefits of it all the time. If you are finding that you are moving in and out of gratitude, check your frame of mind before taking action on anything else.

The article I read in the waiting room that day had a profound impact on my understanding of gratitude and it was a huge relief in my already busy life that I could raise myself into gratitude without effort. As a leader in business you are already busy enough without stacking even more tasks into your life. How it's even possible to make your frame of mind a task is not easy to compute! Sometimes your greatest sense of relief is to know the still spot, which through your open, graceful spontaneity and a quick check of your state of mind, puts the infinity symbol of gratitude ahead of your connection with everything in your world.

CHAPTER 5:
FREEDOM

"Freedom is not worth having if it does not include the freedom to make mistakes." ~ Mahatma Gandhi

Is leading in the 21st century effort or effortless? You hear of just a few incredible leaders at the pinnacle of their success who seem to have an effortless experience. Is this attainable or even real? You see, what I've discovered is that the formula to freedom in leadership is based on something entirely conflicted with the very thought of effort. In this chapter, I share with you the secret to freedom in leadership.

The story of the donkey in the well is a parable from an unknown source. My version of this story is different to the original parable. One day a donkey fell into a very deep dark well. Just as he was about to hit rock bottom he extended his four hooves out to brace his fall. Clinging to the bricks and in darkness he held on for dear life. He was desperate to avoid rock bottom.

The farmer comes along and hears the cries of the donkey echoing out of the well. The donkey is a victim of a terrible event. His cries feel like persecution to the farmer and he berates himself too for not covering the well. The farmer decides that there is no hope and the donkey cannot be saved. He decides to put the donkey out of its misery. The farmer grabs his shovel and starts to fill the well with soil in an attempt to suffocate the donkey. He wants to put the donkey out of his extreme distress and bury him alive. Each time the soil lands on the donkey, the donkey fights with all his might to shake off the sand and frantically digs to keep his head above the soil line. This continues relentlessly for what feels like an eternity. With extraordinary effort and determination the donkey fights off the soil until he starts to move upward toward the light. Eventually, exhausted and crushed by the fight, he emerges victorious and walks out of the top of the well into his ordinary life. He is a survivor and he celebrates the lack of defeat.

This story also has an alternative ending.

The donkey falls fast and then reaching out his hooves clings surprisingly to the brick edges perilously positioned close to what he thinks might be the bottom of the well. He is silent. He goes within. Secretly he is scanning his body and relieved that he has not been broken. He's whole. Deep within his soul he is calibrating and steadying his energy for the inch by inch climb ahead. He will take a solo journey to the top knowing that if it's to be, it will be up to him. Then suddenly something within him gives him a flash of intuition. The voice in his head tells him to let go. Let go of the walls. Trusting this he immediately releases his hooves. He falls fast and the adrenalin in his body is pumping incredibly fast. As if by some magical initiation he is about to learn that at the bottom of the well is a trampoline. He's had magical initiation before and has always celebrated this gift. He hits the trampoline hard. On impact he is bounced with immense energy and whooshes straight up toward the light where the top of the well meets the ground. He flies so fast and so high that he is propelled straight out of the top of the well and high into the sky. In that moment he laughs as he passes his ordinary life. He gets a great view of what his life looked like. At the same time he looks ahead, up and beyond anything he's seen before. He gets an incredible glimpse of the entire universe. The shift in his perspective is massive. The view is incredible. As he lands back on earth, he realises that life will never be the same again. From the courage to let go, he's been given the gift of freedom. He lives an extraordinary life in what is an ordinary place.

When you live your life in a place of integrity to yourself, you need to be able to honestly ask yourself what your ultimate model is -- freedom or struggle? Taking the freedom pathway enables an acceleration of goals achieved, compresses time productively and creates space for fun. It avoids the pressure of over thinking, over striving and the drain of over effort.

Consider though the real meaning of the word freedom. It's the power to act, speak or think as you want. Freedom is self-determination and the quality of being independent of fate or necessity. The effort to have the courage and nothing more than courage to do this and to live in this pace of authenticity creates the effortless slipstream of the elite leader.

I want to unpack the donkey story for you because the layers will help you to understand the place where freedom and the effortless slipstream lives.

In the end of the known version of this story the donkey cries out and feels like a victim. This is the person who blames others for their circumstances. He wants to be rescued. He makes the farmer work hard for his mere survival and yet he cannot work out whether it's good work or bad work. You can well imagine the confusion of having soil thrown at you as a means of getting to the top. How inspired do you feel about leadership that blames others and behaves in ways that disempower choice by harnessing the resources of others by way of drama? The donkey struggles to get to the top and during this struggle he fights everything that is shovelled in his face for the mere outcome of survival.

When he reaches the top his thoughts go to a lack of defeat. There's no celebration. The drama continues.

In the alternative ending are the steps to achieving freedom in leadership and life.

Step one is to be surprised. Look for and anticipate change with an air of surprise. Avoid labelling the surprise as either a positive or a negative. The best freedom comes from simply being open to surprises without labelling them.

Step two is to go within yourself and then look out as though you are sitting inside your own head and looking out your eyes. Imagine for a moment you've shrunk down to being 3 cm tall, and you are inside your own head peering out your eyes as though you are looking out a window with your eyeballs as the window pane. Observe what is happening. Scan, check and be the observer.

Step three is to take ownership. Have the attitude that you own and are responsible as in able-to-respond to all of your circumstances. Know that you have the resources and free will to respond in whatever way you want to.

Step four is to listen to the voice of intuition inside your head. Ask yourself quality questions and answer them in your own mind. A great question is, "how might I have an even better experience of living my authentic self, right now?" Or make the statement, "please send me an awesome flash of inspiration now!"

Step five is to celebrate adrenalin, jitters, excitement, anticipation, a good sweat and other innate responses in new and challenging situations because these responses are the integration of you living your authentic self in your mind, body and your soul.

Step six is to get incredible glimpses by having massive perspective. Widen your peripheral vision as far as you can. Here's a great way of doing this.

EXERCISE: Stand in one spot and start swinging your arms around your body with both arms going left and then both arms going right. Increase the momentum of the movement and then gently add in your head to look over your left shoulder when swinging left and your right shoulder when swinging right. Now look over each shoulder and have an appreciation of 360 degrees of viewing. With your eyes look at the furthest points you can see as you flow in the swinging movement. Then look even further through walls and objects as though you can sense the curve of the earth. Expand your awareness to see even further than you've ever seen before.

Step seven is to choose to live extraordinarily in the ordinariness of life. You have free will and you are able to respond to your circumstances in whatever way serves you. The ability to respond is your own responsibility. Living in the leadership I refer to means you follow what is most exciting for you and expand yourself to find the excitement in everything.

You may be the leader who wants even more than the alternative ending to the donkey story. Perhaps you are a skeptic and want to know what happens if there's nothing to bounce you. I hear you because I've been there, too. I offer you this. The times are rare and pivotal where you do not want the new perspective and you do not want to let go and whoosh so high up that ordinary becomes extraordinary. You have more than enough perspective and you need something deeper. If what I am about to say speaks to your deepest soul, you will remember exactly where you were when you read this.

When you let go and are prepared to fall hard and fast, this moment in time has the power to transform your entire life. Maybe the trampoline will not be there. For me this is so rare that I've only experienced it once.

31

One day I had the experience of the trampoline "not" being there. It was a tough day in a mundane sense because I felt the drama of the experience in human form and an extraordinary day of personal transformation. I describe it as ashes transforming and rising again like a phoenix. I actually had to go through what felt like a complete rewriting of my DNA. I felt like every cell of my soul was being rewritten. This was the day that I realised that humans have the ability to completely transform without needing to die in between.

This is the time you realise that your leadership and your ability to live authentically is so real you are literally the manifestation of the phoenix. From the ashes of unconditional willingness and transformation few leaders will ever experience, you rise into the leader you were destined to be.

The ending to your own donkey story is a multiple choice. The answers are all correct. You have options. Know this, it takes courage and bravery to experience the freefall that leads to the creation of you the leader who is prepared to do what others are unwilling to do.

Next time you feel the pressure of crisis or the opportunity of massive potential ask yourself am I going to fight my way to the top gasping for every last breath? Or, am I going to let go and trust the trampoline will be there without knowing if you will bounce or combust and transform completely. If you have a vision of these possibilities your leadership journey has already advanced in a magical way.

CHAPTER 6:
DRAMA

"The best executive is the one who has sense enough to pick good men
to do what he wants done, and self-restraint to keep from meddling
with them while they do it." ~ Theodore Roosevelt

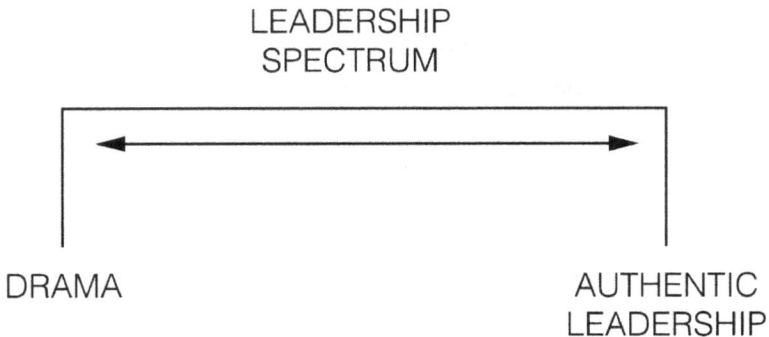

LEADERSHIP
SPECTRUM

DRAMA   AUTHENTIC
                        LEADERSHIP

When I am in the "Vortex of Drama", the exhaustion of drama, the language of drama and the thick oppressive air around drama is so vivid I could photograph it in my mind's eye.

Let me clear the air for you. Drama and leadership have a resonance that is polarities apart and they reside at opposite ends of the spectrum. As a leader, you want to truly excel and releasing all attachment to drama is like letting go of a helium balloon and watching it float to the freedom you've always wanted.

I frequently speak at conferences about drama and leadership. It is a favoured subject for many organisations and I strongly agree that this concept is critical to leadership in the 21st century. In essence, what I am teaching is the **key to living an extraordinary life in an ordinary world.** The ordinary world, particularly in western culture thrives on a good drama. It holds beliefs in place and allows people to justify, find reason, blame and become the hero of the moment. What could be more fulfilling? You may regret asking me this question because leadership devoid of drama is like living in the most successful slip stream of ease and joy imaginable.

Speaking about drama and leadership to groups in the Insurance industry is quite a daunting experience. You see, just about every claim made in the insurance industry is a vortex of stress with its own cataclysmic drama. It would seem, drama is the reason the insurance industry has for being. So you might well imagine that having an anti-drama queen in the room addressing groups whose very existence is drama driven may create some tension. One day it did.

I could see in my peripheral vision the agitation happening in the second row on the left. Wondering to myself will this erupt before or after I finish my presentation, I tuned into the discussion that may come my way in question time.

She was a senior manager and highly experienced in her field. MBA qualified and a group leader in her division. By her own admission she was stressed, adrenal and exhausted. The lump in her throat was probably about feeling humiliated and victimised. Her voice was being projected from a tight spot in her neck so it sounded as though she was only skimming in air and not actually breathing properly. She was trying to find some borrowed energy and with this would save anyone, though perhaps not herself yet. The drama of the ordinary world was harming her.

And she spoke up. As it happened, she has a child with special needs and her husband was retrenched and is now without a job.

In one drama sequence, she saw her son as the victim, the medical system as the persecutor for being so under resourced and unable to help her, and herself as the rescuer who single-handedly needed to save the situation and keep her son alive.

In the next drama sequence, she saw herself as the victim of her husband's lack of work, she was his rescuer because she was paying the bills and his persecutor albeit as the silent assassin because she was fed up with his lack of motivation. Meanwhile, he was playing the victim from being retrenched, he was persecuting his former boss for being insincere and wanted anyone who'd listen to his drama to rescue him.

In the third scenario, her staff were the victims of claimants who were unimpressed by processing and case scrutiny, the clients were persecuting her staff and herself, and due to overwhelm all decisions and progress was piled up on her desk making her fly minute by minute from rescuer to victim herself.

Was it any wonder this woman was exhausted, squeaky voiced and hardly breathing?

Observing her and holding positive energy around her admissions allowed me to see the true value in unpacking drama and providing leadership skills for living in a place that is extraordinary and unaffected by these challenges. It was so exciting to have the chance to work in a remarkable way with someone so courageous that they would stand up in front of the very people she leads to express her distress and her pain.

Drama is a series of events that are highly turbulent, emotional or tragic. In today's world, we are attracted to drama for many reasons. Mostly it gives us significance, an illusion of love and the comparison our emotions need to feel relevant. Our apparent connectedness, which is in so many ways disconnected, heightens our attraction to drama. In the late 1990's, I was working in the Media and Marketing Department for the Sydney 2000 Olympic Games. When the Media Village was occupied there were 2,500 journalists from all over the world in one building. I learnt all about the power of drama from watching the behaviour of media from all over the world. The scandals and injuries, the losses and upsets created the biggest media conferences with journalists rushing to finish the story and frantically storming around the precinct. Other days, where the stories were mild and calm with no drama you'd find the journalists not even bothering to read releases and media conferences empty.

Let me share this with you. Having the resources to move away from drama gives you freedom, vision, accountability, relaxation and happiness. This skill is a key to leadership. It also helps you avoid angst, stress, exhaustion and the feeling of being drained.

There are key steps in creating leadership success through how you respond to and no longer engage with drama.

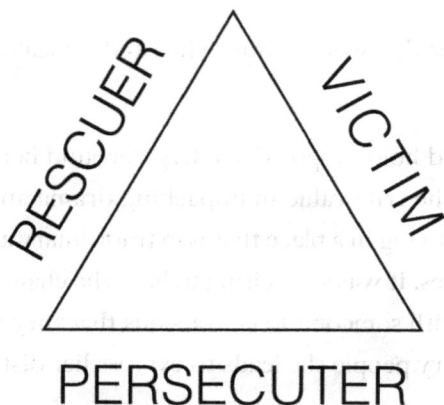

The Drama Triangle used to describe cyclical and habitual roles in co-dependent human behaviour and interactions in psychology and psychotherapy was discovered by Dr Stephen Karpman in 1968.

The model was used in the rehabilitation of relationships impacted by alcoholism and was a foundation to the system used by Alcoholics Anonymous. The Drama Triangle refers to three roles that are often played habitually in enmeshed and un-resourceful interactions. These roles are the victim, the person who persecutes the victim and the person who rescues the victim. The triangle may have one or more persons involved. It's possible to be a victim, persecute yourself and rescue yourself. In a Drama Triangle with two or more participants roles can swap.

Firstly, it's essential to recognise what role you are playing in drama. You may even be swapping roles, so you need to understand what you are doing. Pretend you are watching a movie starring yourself and the drama. As you watch the interactions, as though you are removed and watching a movie, see or imagine the role you and others are playing. Language and emotional state can be a great resource in working this out. The victim often has low energy, feels helpless, does not care for appearances and will have a poor me attitude. The persecutor will be more like a bully, blaming and more aggressive. The rescuer will be the placater, the middleman and the voice of reason.

Still watching the movie you want to look at the result each role is gaining from the drama. This is also known as secondary gain. In human behaviour, the unconscious mind represents 93% of the mind. Your unconscious mind is symbolic; meaning it uses and responds to stories, patterns and representations. Your non-conscious mind also takes everything personally and works on the path of least resistance. By watching the roles within the drama you can assess the gain each participant may be achieving. This may include such things as love, attention, approval, appreciation, forgiveness and/or approval to stay stuck. What's important with secondary gain is that it is a non-conscious behaviour that may look like manipulation, when actually in the mind of the person in the role their intentions are positive. Secondary gain may appear to have benefits, where in reality it's a trap. In leadership, becoming free from this trap is critical to accelerated success.

By watching the drama like a movie you have taken the first step towards resolving the entire drama itself. In effect, you have become the observer and dissociated yourself from the drama. You have removed the immediate emotional charge, even momentarily, long enough to see the drama with peripheral vision and this gives you a wider perspective.

When you are inside the drama, you are what's known as "associated" with the drama. This gives you focussed or foveal vision, like a horse with eye blinker patches on so it can only see through the tiniest of slits. The full picture and all possibilities are hidden when you are associated. The emotional charge feels personal. When you are watching a movie you have a different perspective.

The key to breaking the drama pattern is to be the observer. An observer is a person who watches, notices and monitors something. No action needed. How freeing does it feel to simply watch and monitor!

The final step is to be the creator of what you want, instead of reacting to life. This is achieved by staying outside of drama and you move from watching the movie to being the creator and director of your movie and achieving what you want.

There may be un-resourceful behaviours, and people are not their behaviour so there are no un-resourceful people. The creator is about results, happiness and harmony. Think about leadership and you may have one of your biggest ah-ha moments about drama. Leadership is all about creating. When you create you bring something into existence. What do leaders do? They guide and direct. Leaders are the observers and creators who bring something into existence. This is virtually impossible to do in drama!

Sometimes when you have lots of drama going on it may not be easy to shift into observer and creator with all of them at the same time. In this situation observe your key role. Are you most often the victim, persecutor or rescuer? Then observe your secondary gains as they may be repetitive across several dramas. You can observe your pattern and create a new pattern that may serve you in extracting yourself from many dramas in one go.

I also need to tell you that this one process and shift in you, the leader, can create a shift in the people you associate with. In some cases, you'll find your resonance shifts and colleagues, direct reports, friends and even family with whom your interactions have been almost entirely drama based will drift away. This is something to be celebrated. This shift is ultimately creating space for people with whom you truly resonate with, in a drama-free way, to enter your life. What could be more powerful for you as a leader than to have fully functioning observers and creators hanging around you all the time!

When we finished the session, the brave woman who stood up and shared her stack of dramas at the conference gave me a hug I will never forget. Her life would never be the same again. I've since kept in contact with her and she has progressed in her life like a ton of bricks was lifted from her shoulders. Her son is in a special school and community transport takes him there every day and brings him home in the afternoon. He is being cared for in the way he always needed to be and his behaviours have improved. Her husband found employment and he travels frequently which she says is not ideal and yet perfectly ideal at the same time. She feels more empowered at work, is a more effective leader and has reduced her work hours and overtime due to her productivity gains from being the observer and creator.

If there is one ideal of leadership that creates a massive shift it's the ability to see drama, to observe it and to create what you really want instead. You might tell yourself that in drama you are un-resourceful, and this would be true. You are in charge of your mind and your results so start watching your interactions like a movie and then become the creator and get a sense of what it feels like to be the director of your own life.

CHAPTER 7:
MISTAKES

"Experience is simply the name we give our mistakes" ~ Oscar Wilde

When I first decided to go into business at age 21, I was concerned about the mistakes I would make. It became almost an obsession to hide these from the outside world. My entrepreneur father had told me that 99% of businesses fail in the first 6 years and I was determined to evade this statistic. When I saw mistakes in business for exactly what they really are the distinction transformed my self-confidence and my success. In business, transforming how you feel about and deal with mistakes can be life changing.

One of my mentoring clients, an executive woman, contacted me one day and just a millisecond beyond hello launched into a ballistic unloading. I could almost get a sense of how much she had just spat on her phone handset, she was so incensed. She could not believe the mistakes that were occurring with the tasks her staff were working on. All of a sudden, she wanted everyone to focus on accuracy and in this instance all that was happening were more mistakes. She was upset, angry and felt that every time she tried to address it, things were slipping from bad to worse. In her call to me, she wanted to identify the culprits and decide how to deal with their inadequacies! Her staff had become pensive, frozen and unable to do even the simplest tasks because they were so stressed about the reactions she delivered in relation to their mistakes.

This is a common challenge in businesses both small and large. It is not the "mistake" it's the attitude towards the mistake that can cause a problem. The risks of disempowerment can severely impact a business if mistakes are mistreated by owners and managers.

The question that needs to be answered here is this, what is a mistake really and how can mistakes enable a business to thrive?

A mistake, first time round is a learning experience. It can take you incrementally closer to your business goals in an instance. It is feedback that the way you are going about the task or trying to achieve the desired outcome is flawed. The discomfort of a mistake needs to be motivational, moving away from what you don't want, to instead creating what you'd prefer.

The term mistake, to me on the first account of an action leading to an undesired outcome is a "missed take". Movie directors will repeat the same scene over again until they get the perfect take and everything in between is a mistake. Movie directors have perfected receiving feedback from their missed take. They fine tune, they realign, change angles, get an even better perspective and then they do another take. Retribution, blame and hissy fits are absent. When it comes to fine tuning for the best outcome, the movie industry has it all worked out in filming several takes. It's a creative experiment that can and will be perfected.

To me, every business is a creative experiment that can and will be perfected with the right attitude to learning experiences. When these experiences are viewed as feedback, the business can grow into its success.

When an error of judgement or an action that results in an undesired outcome is repeated, there is definitely a problem that needs to be addressed in the business. Otherwise an action that leads to an undesired result is called feedback.

When it comes to mistakes manifesting into problems in business the following hallmarks are often present:

There is a negative attitude and negative meaning given to mistakes.

With much amusement many of my clients discover that the meaning they give to mistakes is something they have downloaded from childhood and is not serving them as an adult. Many children experience the negative reaction of an adult as they make a mistake, and then label mistakes as "bad." Then in adulthood the natural reaction to mistakes is to see them as "bad." In my business experience, I've recognised that mistakes generally occur at the most fantastic time, and I'm not being sarcastic. Mistakes occur in times of change and growth. So in business, I have always labelled mistakes as, "feedback" and "potential in action." I love and embrace mistakes as a sign of pushing the boundary to the next level of success.

Seeing mistakes as a personal assault and seeking the source for retribution or at the very least a good dressing down.

How does this remind you of your childhood? Being found out, and embarrassed after making a mistake? This is never the best way to build self-confidence and initiative. In business, I see this so often. Management looks for the source, assigns blame and remonstrate the damage, usually in the presence of others. You can imagine the response I receive with the attitude of finding out how the mistake occurred without looking for a person to blame. I look at how it could be prevented or resolved even quicker in the future. I also look to the person who resolved the situation with a view to developing strategies for future effective problem solving management resources.

Determining mistakes are "only" damaging to the business and must be avoided even at the cost of growth.

Certainly mistakes can be damaging to a business, some very much so. What is always critical though is how they are managed and resolved; how staff are empowered to move on and strive to deliver their very best; and how clients and customers affected receive sincere apology and service that goes beyond their expectations as a remedy. This is the power of learning from mistakes and using them as strength. It is unhealthy to attempt to grow a business without the potential to make a mistake. A business will not grow out of fear.

Back to my client, flipping out and losing the plot over her staff and their mistakes. After a few minutes of venting, I wanted to have a clear picture on what making a mistake meant to my client. What were her references and experiences in life about mistakes? Needless to say from a young age she had gained beliefs about mistakes which:

- meant a lack of care

- were a personal attack

- a sign of failure and

- incompetence.

The result was always punishment.

Imagine the barriers to success my client was carrying around with these beliefs? She had never been able to be anything less than perfect. In her moment of clarity, she was gobsmacked at these beliefs and saw how they were not serving her. So I put it to her, what if mistakes are simply, "human potential in action?" She tried it on and for the next few days looked at every mistake as "human potential in action." Dealing with the challenges from this viewpoint enabled her to come up with appropriate and supportive feedback for her staff that motivated them to try a little harder, be fearless in how they tackled the tasks at hand and ultimately saw them break into a new league in the project they were working on.

There are three key mistake-loaded instances where businesses may thwart progress and success by a negative approach to mistakes.

1.   Mistakes being seen as bad.

2.   The need to find and reprimand the culprit.

3.   Create an environment where the staff, fail to strive for growth because of the risk of mistakes being handled in ways that cause stress and upset.

Business success can transform when initiative and action that misses the specific desired outcome is instead viewed as feedback and opportunities for growth. Finding out what your personal references are and what meaning you apply to mistakes may well change the way you manage yourself, others and ultimately determine your success in business now and into the future.

In determining your personal beliefs about the meaning of mistakes the first step is to recall your earliest memories of the consequences of your childhood mistakes. How were they dealt with? What would you have preferred instead?

Next consider some of the mistakes you feel you've made as a business person. How have you remedied these? What meaning have you attached to them? What have you gained from these experiences which have shaped the person you are today? How many apparent mistakes, when learnt from, have actually resulted in a positive outcome?

The third step is to have an honest look at repeated mistakes. These are a problem. The feedback is not being accepted and the learning has been missed. Where in your business are you experiencing the consequences of mistakes on replay? What could be done differently?

Finally is there a blame game culture that you need to address? If yes, then it's up to you to be the change that takes your business in the direction of results instead excuses and reasons. When you are looking to assign blame for a mistake instead of learning from the experience and immediately looking for the best and most resourceful recovery from the feedback gained you thwart progress and slow your achievement of success.

Mistakes are a key part of growth that if immediately learnt from, remedied, labelled as feedback and celebrated for growth can lead to success and happiness beyond measure.

As a child when mistakes are made and how an adult addresses them can leave a lasting impression of them being bad, experiencing retribution and being wrong.

It's time to let this go. The gift of mistakes is that they are actually life enhancing, evidence of progress and can be given a higher meaning.

CHAPTER 8:
WORLD WITHIN THE WORLD

"I think the dual existence thing is a regular pastime for all human beings, and for that matter anything in this universe." ~ Joseph Gordon-Levitt

D ual existence, is this something you are aware of? Have you heard of the world within the world? Let me show you something about leading that you will find interesting.

Every business leader I have ever met has identified that they have a personal world within the world, and they use it to their absolute advantage. By this I mean, you live in the world, that's the tangible place like the chair you are sitting on, the people around you, the buildings you inhabit and the air you breathe. This is the world of which you are very aware. Then there's another world. This world is the world within you. It's your very own world just as vast as the outside world and has within it enormous untapped potential.

When you become aware of the power of your world within the world, your effectiveness in leadership becomes quantum, exponential in nature and effect. You have this resource available to you right now and by switching it on, the influence you have on yourself and others becomes effortless.

I met a CEO of a very large organisation once and noticed that he frowned much of the time we were talking. His business was in crisis, and he was losing the confidence of his board. My sense was that he was lacking trust in his own ability to lead and was looking externally for answers; which I intuitively sensed, he knew within. The deep frown and inward containment of his words were very strong. As is common with executives in high-pressure situations, I sensed he had become so stressed he might just explode; as some in his position do. Recalling this experience, I can almost see a giant Mr Stay Puft, as tall as a Manhattan building, walking down the street in the 1984 movie Ghostbusters (starring Dan Aykroyd and Bill Murray) forging on against every obstacle until he exploded into a million sticky bits of white marshmallow. I see this trait in senior managers of corporations who struggle with effective leadership and think to myself, "Oh no, here comes the marshmallow dude." Thank goodness I'm not being mind-read! It is in this territory that you hear about someone having a heart attack brought upon by work stress. My meeting with the frowning CEO really gave me the vibe of what this candidate looked like in crisis.

As you may have guessed, all I wanted to do was find out what was going on behind that face. I found it fascinating. He was present in the conversation and then at the same time, planning and calculating something else in the background. I could hardly contain myself, so I asked him, "Do you live in a world within the world?" He looked at me in a really puzzled way and then he burst into a deep shade of red. It came up from the collar on his tightly fitted shirt that was being strangled by an ill-fitting neck tie, and filled his entire face, right up to his receding hairline. For a moment, I thought he might burst into tears. I wasn't sure what a 155 cm short, petite female should do when she induces tears in a significantly older, grown man of about 185 cm in stature and almost the same proportions in width. What I did know was this, my words had made an impact. When someone has a sympathetic response in their nervous system to something you've said to them, what tends to happen is that their skin will flush a pink or red. This is a response worth noting.

I took a quick backflip on my line of questioning. Was that what I needed to do? I decided to wait and allow him to process the shift. Within a minute that felt like an hour, he contained his colour and finally he said something. He was intrigued by my question and also confused, so I explained. You see, the greatest leaders I have met have an entire planet inside their mind that they are willing to engage with and bring forward into the outside world in which they live. I explained it to him. What's more, there are specific ways in which you can engage with your inner world to create amazing outcomes in your outer world.

When I think of the world, what comes to mind is the realm that supports life. The outer world that supports life is quite obvious. Your inner world that supports life starts with 100 billion nerve cells in your brain. With these you have neural connections and pathways that create a unique circuitry system that is especially for you. When you experience an external event from the outer world it enters your brain. You cannot possibly take it all in, so what happens is your inner world immediately filters it. It will delete some content, generalise the information and distort it so it becomes more in-line with the current model you have of your life. Your personal model is based on your memories, values, beliefs, attitudes, decisions and life experiences.

In leadership, bringing these two worlds into harmony has many powerful advantages and as the external world we live in becomes increasingly toxic, it's essential that you act. Organised action will move you effortlessly toward your goals; allow you to find more creativity in problem solving; discover answers with ease; and create an inner calmness whenever you like. Today, many leaders talk to me about having fierce determination. Unfortunately, this ends up costing excessive energy and puts pressure on your health. With this fierceness comes a mental block between the outer and inner worlds, enough so to bring on a metaphoric headache!

Bringing these worlds into harmony may allow quiet determination, where results come to you rather than you needing to force or coerce outcomes. You can also reduce stress, reduce feelings of being out of control and move away from living only a small proportion of your true potential by fully understanding and engaging both worlds.

Think about the leaders who inspire you.

- Are they healthy and fit or are they unhealthy and over-weight?

- Do they have great people around them who support them, or do they carry the full weight of all burdens on their shoulders?

- Are they flexible and willing to re-strategise when something goes awry, or do they stay fixed and unbending; refusing to change or admit a mistake?

- Are they respectful of other humans, or do they bulldoze people who might be in their way?

- Do they approach their career as a lifelong journey of learning and expansion, or do they know it all and have a closed mind?

Let me share this with you. It is something intriguingly simple and once you have heard it, completely obvious. The leaders who inspire are healthy, fit, flexible attitude, supported by others and are respectful of all other humans. Leaders want to learn everyday of their life and they are open to receive. Their greatest strength is their willingness to show weakness and to engage the support and brilliance of the people around them, edifying these people all the way. The reason people like them is because they bring the best out of themselves and are able to respond readily because they are grounded within their own life. All of these qualities stem from an inner world which manifests in the outer world. In order to be a great leader, you need to be connected to the values, attitudes, beliefs and decisions of your inner world in a quality way, and then use this connection to motivate a quiet determination to have expansive harmony in your outer world.

I'll show you the steps for creating this powerful and expansive harmony between your inner and outer worlds.

The first step is your accountability for your own physical health. In this regard, it's a matter of showing up in your life as the best version of yourself. I recommend you start with the health of your nervous system because this is the system that controls everything you do. My suggestion for nervous system health is to find a good Chiropractor and have a check-up for nervous system dysfunction or subluxations. This refers to areas within your spine and joints where the messages from your brain are not getting through. If you have nervous system dysfunction, you may or may not have any symptoms. Commonly though, a sign that your body is not coping could be the manifestation of back and neck pain, headaches, stiffness, brain fog, emotional instability and mood swings.

Your physical health is also impacted by your hydration and this means being accountable for how much water you drink on a daily basis. Your brain is 75 percent water. Keeping this functioning at optimal performance levels is essential for leadership, so here's the trick: 70-75 percent of your daily nutrition needs to be water based, not cola based!

Physical activity is essential for the effective performance of your inner world. You may be aware that office workers today spend at least 75 percent of their time at work seated. This translates to 22-23 hours per week. An additional six hours per week is apparently spent sitting in transport. Sitting all day impacts your metabolic rate and lymphatic system, so it's not easy for the body to eliminate toxins and the sluggish feeling can certainly impact your whole state of being, including brain function.

Your flexibility, in the physical sense, is also important on a number of levels. Stretching your body gives your cells oxygen and having good oxygen in your blood stream is essential for detoxification, good metabolism and disease prevention as well as efficient brain function.

Your inner world is the centrepiece of your emotional responses and where you experience your accountability for how you respond to the world. What's interesting about this is that your state of emotion is incredibly influential in your reactions. All reaction really means is a repeated response. I find the word reaction quite amusing, in a clever way, because when you catch yourself re-acting you are simply pressing the human behaviour "replay button" on something you've done before. And if you care to observe yourself, you might just see that you are awesome at it!

So, here's the truth, how you respond to the outer world is 100 percent reflective of the state of your inner world. If you are in an emotional state that is happy, peaceful, measured and flexible, your responses will be happy, peaceful, measured and flexible. If you are beating yourself up in your inner world and feeling angry, tired, upset and inflexible, how you respond to the outer world will be angry, short, sharp, upsetting and rigid. Leader, you already know, no one can make you "do" peeved off! You "do" it and I know it doesn't feel pleasant.

Looking after your emotional health is a daily experience. To achieve a state of emotional harmony is a part of routine and when you make it a habit you have many tangible benefits. Some effective ways to do this include:

- Connect to the energy source of the sun by stepping outside into a place where you can connect to sunlight, directly onto your face. Close your eyes and allow the sunlight to bathe your face for just a couple of minutes. As you do this imagine that the light of the sun and its warmth is entering every cell of your entire body. When the light reaches the soles of your feet, feel it go deeply into the earth below you. You've just filled your inner world with light. This is soothing for your emotions.

- A great way to care for your emotional state is through checking the dialogue you engage with in your inner world. Have empowering questions for yourself when you sense your emotions are negative. One of the best questions you can ask yourself is, "What does my life look like when I am feeling this way?" Then literally ask yourself, "How can I be positive, happy and emotionally flexible right now?" Ask yourself, "Inner world, show me how to do that?"

- An important step in creating expansive harmony between your inner and your outer worlds is to have an experience of what it means to be in flow. Trees anchor themselves to the earth with a strong root system that holds them in place. They have an energy exchange through osmosis and carbon dioxide. When the wind blows, they move with the force, instead of fighting it. Trees have an inner and outer world. They have a secret that every human leader also knows. The secret is this, the person or system with the highest degree of flexibility, controls the system. This is coined in Neuro Linguistic Programming as one of the most convenient assumptions of having harmony and flow. You can use language to increase your flexibility and this starts with asking yourself, "What am I defending?" And then expand this to ask both your inner and outer worlds to help you to understand how you can have both flexibility and your highest ideal in the given situation.

My executive who was under pressure from his board admitted to having an inner world. After we discussed the attributes of inspiring leaders, he agreed that he, in fact, did not embody these virtues in his inner world and it was definitely showing in his outer world. He took steps to restore his health, and although this was not easy for him, he found excellent results that motivated him to commit to the process. He changed his internal dialogue and appreciated how easy it was to be flexible. The most inspiring realisation he had related to the reflection of his emotional state and how suddenly, when he chose to *be* the person who would inspire him, this was reflected in his outer world. Results in the company and productivity improved and in less than one year he and the entire organisation were in a vastly different place to where they were when I met him.

Exploring the power of inner and outer worlds is incredibly important in leadership. You get a sense of how critical your responsibility is to look after your physical and emotional wellbeing and to practice the harmonious flow of flexibility between the dual worlds when you recognise you have both. The reason you have both is because of your design as a leader, so if this feels right, own it and live it.

CHAPTER 9:
SELF-CONTROL

"One morning I woke up and was plunged into psychological shock. I had forgotten I was free." ~ Jack Henry Abbott

There is a dance around self-control and it's spectacular. When you think of self-control, immediately the mind goes to the source of negative behaviours that we want to avoid. Self-control often centres around eating junk food, drinking alcohol, expressing anger or upset emotions. This is the side of self-control that has us persecuting for doing regrettable things. How has self-control crept into total control of expression in business leadership? The reflection is the threat of weakness and rejection.

The other side of self-control is what I want to talk to you about in the area of leadership. In business and corporations today, I see self-control manifested as the stagnation of the worthy and light-filled areas of self-expression and living as an authentic soul. This feels like non-heroic self-control because it's not avoiding something nasty. Instead, it's avoiding something really amazing, something authentic. And what it effectively does is shut down the full expression of your heart and your soul.

How often have you thought of a great idea and then stopped yourself from expressing it? Or decided not to share something because, even though it's incredibly positive, you might squash someone's toes? Have you ever wanted to give someone a big pat on the back and thought, "maybe not, it might be seen as favouritism," or "perhaps someone might get the wrong idea and think I'm being unethical"? You want to say something and you hold it back. This is the most damaging self-control a leader can have!

When I was working in Sports Marketing in the 1990's and early 2000's the environment was incredibly stressful. Deadlines were tight and the line between success and failure was a hair. It's almost ironic really because to make it to the Olympic, Commonwealth and Asian Games, you have to be the best of the best and have some magic that does not come with training alone. It's a gift and a mindset. Working on these events is almost the classic metaphor for the athlete's journey. At the end of the race or when the final whistle blows and you look at the time clock, place board or scoreboard, there's not a second you can add. Not even a one-hundredth of a second you can add to change the result. If you hesitated and made one incorrect move, your games are over and you miss out on the medal.

In the Sports Marketing department is the pressure cooker of revenue. This is the place where the money needs to be made to fund the event. Guarantee as much as possible as early as you can in the lead up, be extremely comfortable with risk, make decisions knowing it will all come down to the final days and minutes. None of this is easy. Bringing in tens and hundreds of millions of dollars and knowing that 75 percent will be achieved in the days of the event itself is stressful. Even something as out of your control as the weather can be the source of winning and losing.

Decisions needed to be made every day, literally like strategic gambling. It's impossible for Managers to make them without the full, 100 percent commitment to absolute precision, heroic delivery and ownership of the entire team. Things just move so fast that one day can create months of future chaos if personal accountability is missing at any level in the organisation.

I found myself one day starting to become overwhelmed by the number and complexity of multi-million dollar decisions that needed to be made. I had incredibly skilled staff and yet the corporate culture was to always have leadership make the decisions. This was just not working for me because the information I was being given was insufficient. I switched it. For every decision, I knew there were options. The proverbial many ways to make light work. So the protocol I developed was for my entire staff to come to me in relation to every decision with three options and three outcomes. The options were their thoroughly considered gold, silver and bronze. The outcomes were their professionally estimated good, bad and ugly. We discussed them and in a place of total authenticity, showing absolutely no self-control in what needed to be said, regardless of how stupid or ignorant or incompetent I or anyone might feel in the process, we showed total positive gratitude for the thinking and the work. If I felt like I truly loved someone for their work and their intelligence you would hear me say, "I love you!" Oh my goodness how politically incorrect of me? Every staff member had to own the options and outcomes presented and had to demonstrate how they would execute them with an all-important deadline. It was incredibly productive to exercise no self-control and I will share the final piece that created ultimate alchemy soon.

Self-control, in the true sense of the dictionary meaning, is to stop yourself from doing something that may not be in your best interests. It is normally associated with negative emotional behaviours, self-restraint, self-discipline and willpower. In 21st century leadership, self-control has crept into virtual total control. This manifests as a withholding of ultimate authenticity, to the point where I meet many leaders who are unable to fully express themselves in ways that are simply awesome. They have difficulty fully showing their own skill and also limit their embrace of others and the brilliance they see around them. The reflection is a feeling of weakness and rejection.

Switching on your ultimate authenticity helps you to bring out the best in yourself and in others. It gives you even more time and space in your day. It gives you energy and reduces brain fog. Ultimate authenticity, expressed through your words, also helps to increase productivity and happiness. Stress reduction is a big positive as it moves you away from second-guessing and internal worry about progress and outcomes.

So here it is leader, **switch on the full, authentic expression of exactly who you are** and focus on what you want to say everyday of your life. This is a key to 21st century leadership. Bring it into the positive. If it's negative, ask yourself "What do I want instead?" Answer this question in your mind before you open your mouth. Then express what you want and edify everyone around you to bring forth the most incredible magic in their life every day. This is your number one priority. Speak to their highest ideals of who they take themselves to be. In the positive, in what I refer to as the light, show them *their* light, qualities, best outcomes, wins, gains, areas to grow and develop, and highest ideals. Even when you want to mentor, coach and pull them up on their failings, your job is to bring this into light for them and switch off the self-control that inhibits the positive aspect of your authenticity. When you use authentic leadership you can even give someone a professional strike or warning by showing them up in a positive way and making them aware of what you know they are truly capable of, and are perhaps unwilling to do. If they check out, sit in the ejector seat and have to leave the organisation – this is okay.

Ways to increase the flow of authentic communication in your leadership include:

- Create an appreciation list and add to it every day.

- Start meetings with edification and positive statements about individuals.

- Use the question, "Can I share?" and then, with consent, be fully authentic when you speak.

Present opinions that may be controversial with the statement, "This may not land well and..." Remember to always use "and" to join this statement with your comment as using "but" or "however" negates what is said in the first part of the statement. For a more detailed discussion of this practice, see Chapter 11 on Ideas.

Use strong positively emotive words like love, adore, magic, awesome, amazing, and perfect in your conversations to inspire people.

Give your people a voice and let them make decisions that are well considered.

Give credit for ideas and actions to the individuals responsible.

Support the process when something goes awry. Take a solutions based approach to problem solving and positively empower the individuals responsible to progress to the outcome sought.

In the beginning, you may find that people are unsettled by your new approach and your fluid authenticity. Keep it going! The process of shifting takes time, and just as you need to settle into anything new, you need to be consistent to gain the results you are looking for.

The final piece that created the alchemy in my Sports Marketing roles was incredibly powerful and, I feel, crucial to the success I achieved in leading my teams. Knowing that the road from A to B is never straight and often results in unexpected outcomes, my commitment to them was solid. As long as decisions were based on the co-creation of our collective expertise and opinion, they were always guaranteed of my 100 percent support. Even if the outcome was not as expected, a decision proved to be flawed or we needed to divert the entire project. My team was assured of having my 100 percent commitment to being by their side for the new directions and actions needed. This commitment is the most incredible safety net a leader can give their team and the one that ultimately has everyone rise to greatness that is beyond measure.

Your self-control is monumental when you let go of attachment to the control and are able to express your authentic self in the light. When you continuously and purposely use this positive side of your role as a leader you will feel the quantum growth in your capacity to co-create incredibly powerful outcomes.

CHAPTER 10:
PHYSIOLOGY

"A leader is a dealer in hope." ~ Napoleon Bonaparte

Have you ever walked into a room and sensed, just by hearing someone's voice or looking at them, that they are a leader? There's a certain physiology that goes with leadership and you can achieve this every time you choose to. I adopt different physiologies depending on my environment all the time.

Two of the businesses that I now own are in the healthcare sector. One is a clinic in Sydney employing six Doctors, and the other is a Business Optimisation & Marketing Consulting enterprise. Through the latter, I train Doctors in client rapport and communication skills, and create exclusive, individually branded health information and client education materials for clinics.

One day, I was coaching a young female Doctor who was having challenges establishing herself in practice. She felt her colleagues and patients saw her as quiet and lacking in confidence. It impacted her to such a degree she was contemplating whether she should continue to work in the profession at all. She was struggling to the point of despair. At university, her grades were amazing and she graduated with honours and a university medal.

As a petite woman myself, with a small voice and a diminutive personality, I felt certain I could help her. What was even better was that being just 155 cm short myself, I could get a definite sense of how she might be feeling. All of her colleagues were physically bigger than her, including an alpha male and an alpha female who were giants in comparison. My young Doctor was an apologiser and a giggly woman who was not being taken seriously. The challenge was in her physiology and this I could help her with.

Physiology is the study of how an organism works. When I refer to the physiology of leadership I am referring to how someone stands, looks, feels within himself, breathes, speaks, listens and interacts when in a leadership state of being.

To understand the physiology of leadership, it's essential to realise its importance. We are all energy beings. Everyone knows the experience of walking into a room and feeling that you could cut the air with a knife. You may hear people refer to someone as being great to be around. Others will refer to a leader as being dependable, solid, trustworthy, honourable, articulate, with a presence or strong. It is their energy blueprint that you are recognising in these traits and it is something you feel, hear and see.

When you create your own energy blueprint for the leader you are:

- You feel even more confident, speak to anyone with ease, address groups and participate in public speaking.

- You readily gain the confidence of clients, co-workers and management.

- It gives you valuable skills in making effective personality assessments, while avoiding the pitfalls of misreading people.

- You develop the physiology of leadership that helps you avoid feelings of being shy and reserved and will help you avoid missing out on promotions and opportunities to progress in your career.

When I was studying to become a Trainer of Neuro Linguistic Programming, my mentor and clinical supervisor Pip McKay, gave me her e-book, "How to Prevent your Child from being Bullied." This book is based on the hierarchy of status that she created in the 1990's. Pip originally developed this hierarchy when she taught acting to children and adults. It is a process I use to assist Managers and CEO's find the physiology that most reflects how they want the world to receive them or what they display when their personal protection portal, or cylinder, is opened (see Chapter 13, Cylinder). Not only is this helpful for individuals to be aware of, its relevance to leadership is crucial in the 21st century.

In the analysis, Pip talks about a hierarchy of eight status levels, all of which have accompanying physiology.

Negative - The lowest is the "loser" or "whiner," whose type will say what other people may want to say, and don't. You might think of them as having no filter, in a negative way. They also complain.

Invisible - The next level makes them invisible. I've had this type in my trainings and when they approach me afterwards, I've hardly remembered them at all. They are quiet and reserved, pulling their energy in. When I want to be invisible I imagine I'm the size of a green pea! It's quite effective, especially when I'm running to the gym on a bad hair day, with no makeup on. I want to be anonymous. Not such a good idea when leading in business.

Apologiser - Some people I mentor fall into the next category, of saying sorry all the time and getting walked all over. They say sorry all the time so their status is the apologiser.

Helper - The next level is also unhelpful, despite being helpful. This person is kind and just wants to help other people. They have sympathy for everyone and they'll have a story to match your sad and sorry ones every time. The challenge is, that empowerment is not easy to achieve when you are busy allowing others to be un-resourceful.

Follower - We all know the followers who copy, without effect, and agree all the time.

Social Organiser - Being a great social organiser although relevant at times, has the potential to be distracting and again, of little benefit as a leader.

Bully - How many bullies do you know who think they are leaders? Do you like them? They are inflexible and always need to win an argument. I am no fan of bullies in business and given that most people find blaming behaviour off putting, it's little surprise when real leadership is called for – everyone dislikes the bully and their antics.

Leader - To me, this is the level of ultimate flexibility and vision. When you truly own this physiology in every cell of who you really are you have a calmness that literally says, "I honour whatever shows up." The filter is off.

So you can see, you the leader have a physiology. Leaders have a natural intelligence and authority which is displayed in a calm and self-assured way. You the leader must be prepared to have a thorough knowledge of your field. More than knowledge, you must be prepared to confidently apply theory to situations in a creative manner and be expansive in your continued learning. I call this a "lifetime of learning" journey. Leaders can seem aloof and be hard to relate to. If you find your leadership style is that of a thinker and this thoughtfulness makes you appear aloof, ensuring you come from a place of appreciation and good intentions can help to counteract this perception. Like many leaders I know, you may live in a world within a world (see Chapter 8, World Within a World). This means you may come across as aloof, when really, what you are doing is listening to your inner dialogue.

The voice of you, the leader, comes from the ground beneath your feet. When you bring your voice up from the ground beneath you it has a resonance which is calm, strong, discerning and powerful. Have you ever heard managers who squeak when they speak? Their voice is being squeezed out of a tiny hole between their neck and their mouth, which started in their throat with a great big lump. They give you little confidence and become irritating to listen to.

When you, the leader, stand - you are still. You'll notice no flapping of your arms or hands. Your movements are deliberate and obvious. You'll sense an invisible string keeping your head and neck aligned and poised. When you've truly adopted your physiology and have certainty, you sense your peripheral vision is so wide you have eyes in the back of your head.

True leaders have flexibility and can occupy different status positions. As I mentioned above, I have times when I truly want to be invisible and I will pretend I'm the size of a green pea. I am also required to be social in my business and personal life, so I can adopt the social organiser role when I need to and busily host a function, make social introductions and plan an event. Even when I am presenting, the need to step out of leader-mode can arise and I will find ways to relate to someone's troubles and be a sympathetic ear to a client who needs to be heard. If I'm tired, I am fine to be a follower at the end of a busy day, and will go with the flow and follow the group to dinner or drinks. We all flow between the different status levels. The choice you need to make though is where you spend your time when you are deliberately choosing to lead.

If you are developing your physiology as a leader and have not gained the response you are looking for, check-in to make sure you are not being a bully or a sympathiser. These are the two status levels I find are most confused with leader. Interestingly enough, the bully is also the persecutor in the drama triangle and the sympathiser, the rescuer, so you can appreciate how our physiology impacts us in drama too (see Chapter 6, Drama).

My young female Doctor realised immediately that her constant apologising and cute personality was ill-fitting for her role as a caregiver for human life in crisis. We worked on her posture, stance, eye movements, hand gestures and her voice volume, tone and pitch. Through this work she became grounded and had a new resonance. She felt more confident in her job and had authority. Her colleagues and patients took her more seriously and she started to receive referrals she had never had before. Her patient base doubled within four months.

Seeing your physical presence as a means of demonstrating your leadership is a key to how others receive and perceive you. As a leader, this is fundamental to your role and position. The feeling of leadership is a key to going forward with natural authority and the air of intelligence, which is essential for your business success in the 21st century.

CHAPTER 11:
IDEAS

"No idea is so outlandish that it should not be considered with a searching but at the same time a steady eye." ~ Winston Churchill

The essence of leadership begins with what you hear when your mind delivers you an idea. When you own the world inside your head, you can transform the messages you receive into actions in the world outside your body.

Some people have expressed to me that they never have ideas. You might be one of them? Ideas are not always easy to recognise. Is there a difference between mind chatter and ideas or are they the same thing? For some people ideas are a feeling or a hunch. Others have a voice inside their head that speaks to them. Other people see images and pictures inside their head or daydream in pictures. You might sometimes get a sense that your mind is simply off wandering somewhere and you are off with the pixies so to speak. It may be that you compute and calculate thought processes in your brain. This is where your leadership begins.

Recognise each of these internal processes as an idea. The start! Instead of calling it an idea maybe think of the chat as concepts, messages, higher self-connection or intuition. Whether designed for your safety or your advancement, it's all worth accepting in some capacity.

Leadership is delivered firstly from recognising an idea and then unpacking your ownership of these hunches, dialogues, images and internal processes.

Ideas are the starting point of leadership because they represent a guiding force that enables you to be the creator of what you are seeking. They come from a place of quiet wisdom and are designed to help you grow. The challenge is that many people become confused about the voice inside their head and they dismiss and/or self-criticise the ideas that flow from innate wisdom.

In the 21st Century, owning ideas and manifesting them into realities in leadership has become increasingly more challenging. Through technology, the pace of information we are exposed to renders many people into a state of being unable to differentiate between mindless mind chatter and quiet wisdom. Then when expressed in an outward manner, many would be leaders are met with feedback that may create an uncertainty wobble. Too many experiences of having ideas critiqued in ways that create a sense of rejection may lead to a shutdown of idea expression. Yet, the essence of all great leadership comes from having the confidence to express ideas frequently and openly, receiving feedback in a discerning manner and staying on purpose. Often times they need to be forthright and measured regardless of the opinions of others.

I once had a client who was creative and brilliant in her field and at the same time unfulfilled and often times vulnerable and stressed. One day, I noticed that she had a rubber band on her wrist. She always wore beautiful jewellery so the rubber band was out of place. I asked her about it and at first she resisted my enquiry. As it happens, she used the rubber band to flick her wrist and cause herself pain whenever her inner thoughts come into her conscious mind. I wanted to understand how this was assisting her in her life. I mean, could all of her inner thoughts be negative? Surely there were some goodies in there too? She said to me that her mind chatted to her all day long and that most of the chatter was distracting. She wanted it to go away and leave her alone. When I went a little deeper into her experiences with ideas it was really that she had felt rejection for her self-expression and did not want to endure this anymore. She needed some resources to assist her because in these beliefs hid her greatest potential.

Are all of the thoughts that pop into your mind destructive? No, I doubt it, because the brilliance of leadership is the ability to take your ideas and manifest them into something a follower is unwilling to do.

The first ideal of leadership is to own your ideas and by this I mean own all the thoughts that pop into your conscious mind without blocking and judgement. This is the first brilliance of leadership and by creating this flow the essence of your ability to move yourself forward and take others with you becomes available.

What is an idea and how do I define it?

Any thought that pops into your conscious mind is an idea. You don't need to pass any judgement, good or bad. What you do with the idea is what makes all the difference. You see idea stands for I Decide Every Action. Thoughts are ideas that are available for you to be discerning with and to make choices. Behind every idea is your choice to decide to do with it what you want. This is how I define the concept of every idea.

Our ideas assist us to grow in all areas of our life. They can bring us self-confidence, happiness, joy and they inspire us which inspires others. Ideas can also help us out of a rut, identify un-resourceful behaviours and show us where we are off track.

Earliest philosophers believed that the ability for someone to create and understand the meaning of ideas was an essential and defining feature of human beings. The word idea originated in Greek with the meaning coming from the root of *idean* which means "to see."

What are the steps to owning your ideas then?

Step 1: Let them through

The first step is really simple. Let them through! Regardless of the meaning you attach to your ideas, what's behind the word idea is the protection I have afforded you right now: I as in you, decide every action. You are fully in charge of your own mind and your own thoughts. Therefore, you are also in charge of how you use your thoughts and consequently your ideas. Your thoughts and ideas are actually nothing without action and since you decide every action there's nothing an idea can do to unstick you in any way. I assure you leader that no one is actually mind reading you right now, so you have nothing to be concerned about in the flow of letting your ideas and chatter be a part of who you really are.

Step 2: Unpack your ideas

Next, learn how to unpack your ideas. The fastest way to learn about your own mind and it's ideas is to have 2 small notebooks nearby. My mentor and dear friend Julie Lewin taught me this technique and I highly recommend it. You will need one red and one green notebook. For seven days every time you have either mind chatter or an idea check in with how you feel about it. If it makes you feel happy, alive and excited, write it in the green book. If it makes you feel upset, annoyed or drained write it in the red book. After seven days, review both books. You might find your inspiration is in the green book, and your negative thought processes are in your red book.

One of my favourite actions to enable the ownership of ideas is to "people watch" with internal commentary. What's even better is internal commentary which you then verbalise in the moment. My best experiences of this have been with a close friend of mine in a public environment and I'm willing to admit I once did this for 5 hours one day while relaxing on the grassy hill overlooking Bondi Beach in Sydney. You can easily do this on your own though and it's a great way to start allowing your ideas to flow and for your nervous system to have a good experience of how positive this action really is. If you've never done it, then you are in for one heck of a fun experience. So what you do is this, you simply watch people and you think about what they may be thinking in their mind and you verbalise it. Try to be as real as possible to how they think as you observe them. So for me, this is always going to be hilarious. It does not need to be sensible, it just needs to demonstrate a connection between your mind chatter and your ideas and then express them.

Here's an example:

"See that family over there? Dad's about to lose it! He's just arrived at the beach and his kid needs the toilet. It's a 20 minute walk on the hot sand."

What this exercise helps you do is realise where ideas and thoughts come from and gives you the power to be creative and own them in a safe environment. The more you have a positive experience of flowing thoughts into words, the easier it will be to own your ideas and bring them forward into your leadership. This is really powerful in 21st Century leadership and you'll recognise that the most inspiring leaders today have an ability to do this.

Step 3: Embrace confusion

You might be interested to learn that embracing the confusion in your mind is the next step to owning your ideas. When it comes to ideas, confusion is a positive sign. What I've learnt about confusion is that it is critical to leadership and to manifesting great outcomes through your ideas. Confusion enables our mind to process and learn. By learning you gain greater insights which can lead to an even more successful outcome. Over many years, I observed leaders become agitated and frustrated when confused and what I love is the critical timing of this emotional state. From now on, your new understanding about confusion is that it's one of your greatest strengths. Confusion is simply your non-conscious mind asking a very simple question. The question is, "Can you help me to understand?" Every time you feel confused about an idea or a thought all you need to do is say to yourself, "Can you help me to understand?" This opens your non-conscious mind, which is 93% of your entire mind, to be gently guided to an answer that eliminates the confusion you feel.

Step 4: Use language that supports you

The final step in owning your ideas is to bring them forward with language that will support you all the time. Many leaders find this action obliterates the sense of rejection around ideas and allows confident expression of what you may judge in your own mind. Preface every idea with the words, "This may not be a good idea and...." Let me deconstruct this for you. The non-conscious mind does not process negatives so when you say to someone, "may not be a good idea" the non-conscious mind hears the words, "good idea." That's all! It does not hear the "may not" part. So you have created safety around your idea. I love starting sentences with this language because the space created literally means you cannot feel rejected.

Next, it is really important to use "and" before you express what you want to say. What the "and" does is connects your idea to "good idea." For example, if you used "but" or "however" instead of "and" you've shot yourself in the foot because "but" and "however" make negative whatever you say next. Let me give you an example which is unrelated to ideas so you get what I am referring to as a simple language tool. Here's a statement for you to consider:

"You look great *but* your hair is a mess."

How does that feel? Do you feel great when someone says you look great but your hair is a mess? The looking great part seems insincere when the "but" steps in right?

Instead, what if they said:

"You look great *and* your hair is a mess?"

How does that feel? Does it negate the looking great part? Instead it just gives you something to feel even better about doesn't it?

So here's an example with both parts of this language tool and an idea at work:

"This may not be a good idea and I think we should reconsider working with that client."

Wow! How controversial of you to lead the way and consider that choosing clients is a good business decision. By the way, I love how you think because choosing clients instead of doing business with just about anyone is actually leadership brilliance in my mind.

Read the statement again. Did you connect with good idea? Did you then flow into validating the idea?

How does presenting it in this way feel by comparison?

"I have an idea, let's dump that client."

Out on a limb? Your idea set up to fail?

Language can make a huge difference when it comes to supporting yourself when you want to share your ideas without risking rejection. In leadership, this is critical because you are going to need to be great at expressing your ideas as a skill in 21st Century leadership.

My brilliant creative client who flicked her wrist with a rubber band each time her mind chatted to her or a thought popped through, confidently started using these simple steps to be discerning and own her ideas instead of punishing herself. She found it liberating and it gave her confidence to accept feedback without feeling like it was a failure. She is also well versed now in appreciating which of her thoughts energise her and which of her thoughts drain her so she has choices when she checks in with her own mind. For her, the one skill that has made all the difference is the sense of confidence she has with the protection behind ideas, being, "I decide every action." My client has been so successful with her shift in relation to ideas that she has been promoted at work and has increased her influence in her social circles.

How you see your mind chatter and ideas and listen to your inner voice is critical in leadership. The greatest leaders of our time are ideas people like you, and they have skills in filtering through their mind's messages to determine what will serve them. With this in place you have flow and simple to use resources to go for it and be confident with expressing your ideas.

CHAPTER 12:
DIFFERENT

"Being different and thinking different makes a person unforgettable.
History does not remember the forgettable." ~ Suzy Kassem

In my business and on leadership the sense of peace I have around the word "different" is liberating. I listen to this word in my mind every day of my life. As a leader, you will see how this simple word transforms your experience of leadership and gives you untold freedom to truly have an advantage in leadership and in life.

In early 2002, I was drawn to the Avatar program created by Harry Palmer. The first step in this program was a weekend course, onto which could immediately be added, two further steps that made it a ten-day program. The timing was challenging, I'd never been away from my partner for more than a few days since we'd met and I would be away on his birthday, something that felt wrong. I needed to be brave and take a step into the unknown and when I did I decided to go straight into the full ten-day program. I travelled from Sydney to Byron Bay to attend the program at the home of the certified facilitator.

I was very nervous. I had decided to do this program at a very challenging time. Visibly pregnant, and on the globally harrowing day of 11 September 2001 when the world lost so many innocent lives due to the terrorist attacks in the US, my unborn child passed away. I want you to know that today I am the mother of two beautiful healthy children. By sharing my experience in 2001 with you in this context, I want you to have an understanding of the magnitude of the heaviness of this time both personally and globally. What I was struggling most with was a battle of right and wrong. On a deeper level, it was a battle of blame and accountability. What I really wanted was to release judgement and appreciate that it is only the perception of the individual that dictates whether something is really right or wrong. For me this was about finding the victim and the perpetrator and maintaining the knowledge that the beliefs about right and wrong live deeply entrenched in the drama triangle that I frequently refer to. The resource that I discovered in this space inspires balance in my life every day and has assisted me immensely.

Defining "different" is the key to unlocking blame. Different means distinct and separate. It creates an opening to seek to understand two sides, and a knowing that the two sides are opposites. What "different" also does is removes the emotion of blame, right, wrong and the need to define one outcome or circumstance as better, or more noble than another. They are simply "different" to each other.

When an emotional charge comes up and the mind seeks to find right and wrong, it is perfect timing to simply stop and allow the word "different" to enter your consciousness. The calmness of "different" releases the stress and angst of taking sides and of trying to find reason. Employing this concept at such a time brings clarity, balance and the ability to look peripherally at circumstances and situations without judgement, providing incredibly valuable vision for you as a leader. It takes you away from assigning sides or risking emotionally charged decisions in the moment and allows for space to consider.

This approach to dissolving the emotional charge between right and wrong, to instead view the differences, is at the cornerstone of mediation. When used with intention, it can serve as a form of immediate and personal leadership mediation to resolve judgement whenever it arises. Mediation is intervention in a process or dispute to bring about a resolution. The principle of mediation involves reviewing the matter in a neutral and independent way, establishing the differences and then seeking to have each side understand and be understood by the other. This approach dates back to Ancient Greece and then Roman law in 530 BC, where mediators were referred to, amongst other names, as "interpres" meaning interpreter.

The steps to working with the word and concept of "different" can become involuntary when you practice the steps from **trigger** to **resolution.** This learned skill in leadership can be defining and incredibly powerful. This can be very helpful in business and in leadership.

First, notice any emotionally charged situation where you want to either find right and wrong or you want to label victim and perpetrator. This is the trigger you are looking for to apply the new thinking.

Second, allow the word "different" to come into your consciousness. Rest with "different" and allow it to rise above right and wrong, victim and perpetrator.

Third, in your mind or on paper, make a simple list, without thinking in any detail about what is different about the two sides. You are comparing what you feel in the moment is right, and what you feel in the moment is wrong, by expressing the thoughts as, "different to each other."

In this exercise, when you feel emotionally charged, the action to take is to ask yourself what is "different." It is much easier to see both sides when you compare them in this manner and by simply defining the differences, the emotive wording changes its charge and becomes more objective.

The fourth and final step is to absolve the judgement. The easiest way to do this is to ask yourself, "What were all of the best intentions in the situation."

I am often brought back to the presuppositions of this statement. The assumption is that everyone does the best they can with the resources they have available, and as a result of this, the behaviour in question is motivated by a positive intent.

In step four, what I mean is for you to consider standing in the place of all aspects, to consider the intentions from a position of difference rather than judgement, and to release the emotional charge by labelling each position as nothing more than "different."

CHAPTER 13:
CYLINDER

"Could we change our attitude, we should not only see life differently, but life itself would come to be different. Life would undergo a change of appearance because we ourselves had undergone a change of attitude." ~ **Katherine Mansfield**

People are not easy to read. If you think this, then truth be known, you are not easy to read. How you show up, in your authenticity, determines how you might be read by others. What you see in others, you may well be denying in yourself. You see, most leaders I meet walk around with a magnificent cylinder around themselves. I call this cylinder a "personal perception portal." It's about a metre from your body and it encases you 360 degrees from head to toe. It has doors at the front like elevator doors, and generally, you think no one can see or feel it! These cylinders are used by the person inside in several ways. In this chapter, you will learn about these cylinders, determine whether you use one and have the opportunity to see other inhabitants of cylinders around you in a whole new light.

Your ability to cope with feedback is essential for your effectiveness as a leader. Call it criticism, call it praise, call it your failings - all of it is just feedback. I am referring to the expression of how other people perceive you and your actions. This may not be easy to swallow... but how other people perceive you, is **something that they control.** Leader, you'll be even more effective when you let go of your self-perception! I am frequently asked the question, "Who am I as a leader?" People want to know who they are or who they are meant to be, as a leader. The answer is, and will always be this: Who you are as a leader is subjective and no matter how you show up, fake or authentic, you have absolutely no control over how other people perceive you. Take the filter off. Who you are is what someone, everyone, else feels and sees in your presence. This is who you are. Take this as a gift of freedom.

I love giving leaders the example of coming across a dog in the street. If you and I were walking together and we came across a big dog, I would be scared. You might look at me and think, "Crikey, that cute puppy could not harm a flea!" Who's right and who's wrong? I'm in fear. You're in puppy heaven. Your experience of the dog is that he's harmless, this is how you perceive him and you are 100 percent right. My experience is that I'm scared, he might be vicious, and my experience is also right. We are both right! Consider this with people.

- Fake or authentic? You decide.

- Like or don't like? You decide.

- Scary or harmless? You decide.

How people receive you has absolutely nothing to do with you and everything to do with them. You might say I'm a completely genuine, likeable and harmless person and hey, some people might feel the same way about you. Others will not, but either way, their beliefs about you have nothing to do with you.

Knowing this, you now have a choice. How are you going to show up? Fake or authentic?

One day, I was called into a large organisation that was having communication challenges between staff members in one of their departments. They asked if I might be able to find out what was going on and help the staff to get along and be more productive. I first spoke to one of the Executive Assistants. I often speak to EA's because many are future leaders hiding in a cylinder of, "I'm not enough yet." Many are incredibly skilled with great collaboration, insight and peripheral vision and usually they know a tonne more than they give themselves credit for. The EA spoke to me about how she felt the department Manager was aloof and not easy to read, and then would become charming in a way that could not be trusted. He would give the illusion that he was interested in the opinions of his team and then when they opened up to him, he was not trusting and would find a way to ridicule or disempower them. She said it seemed as though the minute he drew you in and you thought you were getting close to having his respect, you'd get a sense that you were being set up to have all of your shortcomings exposed, while he kept his aloof distance and watched you fail. She was often asked to write reports and felt she could no longer use her initiative, because even though he gave her the authority to write the report, he rarely considered them good enough when completed. She could not gauge the results he was after and his criticisms were petty.

I wanted to know about her field of protection and how she was using it. As a result of her experiences with her Manager, I was guessing that she may be hiding her full potential inside a self-imposed cylinder. My sense was right. She explained to me how she kept to herself and tried to second guess how to behave and interact in the office. Was she being her authentic self? No. Did she feel it was making any difference to be fake? No. She was stressed and upset and I had a sense that everyone else in the office might be feeling the same. My role at this point was to empower the human soul in front of me instead of taking this information to the Manager to sort him out! This takes us right back to the question of, "Who am I?" The Executive Assistant needed to know that her Manager was a projection of her own reality, and that by changing herself, her experience of him would also change.

In my discussion with her, I explained that having protection around yourself is very important, and yet within it, you need to be authentic and you need to work out how best to show up in the world. A cylinder is for safety, which is one of the prime directives your unconscious mind requires each day of your life. As a leader, you need to have the skills that enable you to be effective and authentic, and to have and use a cylinder at the same time. This made sense to the Assistant and she was ready to receive these resources.

Let me define the cylinder and your personal perception portal for you. A cylinder is a solid geometrical figure with straight sides and a circular or oval base and lid. The space between you and the sides, base and lid of your cylinder, is pure white and quite bright. Most leaders live in these portals for personal protection and status. Visualise it being a metre wider than you on all sides and a metre higher than you. Although the brightness makes it feel very open, it's sealed at the top and bottom. You have doors, like lift doors, at the front. If you want to have a good laugh about cylinders and get a picture in your mind, think back to the Mork from Ork pod in the 1970's/early 1980's sitcom, "Mork and Mindy," starring the late Robin Williams. My imagination is so vivid, and my sense of humour so unfiltered, that sometimes when I meet leaders in cylinders they remind me of Mork, and I have to stop myself from greeting them with "Nanu Nanu!"

How you use your cylinder is determined by what you "send out" from your safe space to others and how close you allow people to come to you. In other words, it is what you allow others to perceive. Perception is your intuitive recognition of events or actions based on what you feel, hear and see. The portal is the gateway you create in your cylinder that lets people feel, hear and see you, whether that be your authentic or fake self. You open and close this portal, allowing people to see your human soul, at will.

I like that you have a cylinder around you and I think you should keep it. The reason is that it protects you. It keeps your energy high, gives you the freedom of personal space, allows you to observe other people and situations from a distance, and gives you a safety valve. You choose who gets close to you emotionally and physically, and this is really important. Your cylinder protects you.

Whilst having many positive qualities, the cylinder of a leader may also act as a blockage to authenticity. It can be a hiding place, and in some cases, I've noticed that some people use their cylinder for some weird behaviour (such as silent treatment, projecting emotions onto others while seemingly uninvolved and aloof, secretly watching another's actions without being visibly present), which in essence, becomes a test of strength and conviction for everyone who comes close to them.

There are some important steps to the effective use of your personal cylinder and its portal in leadership.

Firstly, own up to it! If you have a personal protection cylinder that surrounds you and keeps the real you separate from others, that's okay.

Secondly, recognise and appreciate it so you can begin to understand how it might affect you. Think of the positive ways in which distance from others is good for you. Your cylinder is probably good for maintaining your energy levels, being discerning, making others around you accountable, having vision, introspective thinking and planning. Outside of leadership, how is your cylinder effective in other areas of your life? Consider your relationships, family environment, friendships and health.

Thirdly, really have an honest sense of how it may disadvantage you and others. You may use it to block your authenticity, which gives people misconceptions about you. You may distance yourself from standing by your leadership decisions or prevent yourself from connecting in positive ways to the people who support you. Outside of leadership, does your cylinder prevent you from having the closeness you look for in your intimate relationship and friendships? Do you use it to disconnect from personal responsibilities?

Lastly, decide how you want to use this cylinder in even more effective ways. How are you going to use the portal and deliberately switch it open or closed? When you realise you are always protected by your portal, you can appreciate that being authentic all the time only has an upside. Get a sense of what your life looks like when you are authentic all the time and have this field of bright light protection around you. It's available for you, whenever you need it.

You may have had the experience of meeting someone for the first time and disliking them, and years later, as dear friends, laugh and laugh about that first encounter because it was such a contrast to the deep affinity you now hold for the other person. This is how the EA now feels about her Manager. With the resources of knowing about how she was showing up in her cylinder in the workplace, and how her Manager was doing the same thing, the EA was able to show herself some kindness and cut herself some slack. At the same time, she was able to be more resourceful with the behaviour of her Manager, and receive his feedback, knowing she was protected. Most importantly, she was able to recognise her own authenticity and the boundaries she needed in order to reduce her personal stress toll.

Seeing the cylinder described like this may give you an insight into the game of push and pull within leadership. Having a sense of how to use this protection mechanism for maximum positive outcome is a skill that can be mastered and one that will provide you with the freedom to show up in the best way possible, in every circumstance imaginable. To know your non-conscious drive for safety is always there for you is an incredible resource for any leader in the 21st Century.

CHAPTER 14:
EMPATHY

"No one cares how much you know until they know how much you care." ~ Theodore Roosevelt

In business, leadership empathy is an important skill. In this chapter, I share the story of one of my mentoring clients, a strong burly executive who loves to think that the world sees him as being, "as rough as guts!" In his work and business, he had always felt that being empathetic was a sign of weakness until he discovered it was a key strength. Even so, he had little idea on how to show empathy.

I could feel from the moment I answered the call from him one day that something had dropped. I knew by the scratchy voice with an audible lump being swallowed. On the line was my mentoring client, an executive with the preferred nickname bulldog. Everyone called him bulldog. He accepted no title other than bulldog. I had wondered after working with him for more than a year whether it was a name given to him for appearance or on account of his behaviour. Right now on the call that did not matter. What I saw in this moment was no bulldog. I saw someone who had the softness of a puppy and I could not wait to find out why.

Bulldog is working on a major restructuring project involving personnel and resources across a wide geography. Typically, he is assigned these roles for his pragmatic take no prisoner barrier to getting the job done. His company is a large multi-national. The culture is loud and boastful and in working with him I have always found entertainment and plenty of rough attitude.

He was finalising the implementation of the restructure and on this day he'd met a group of young workers for the first time. Normally, he would just say what needed to be said and move on. Today was proving to be different, gut wrenchingly so. Using skills of sensory awareness, rapport and a deeper listening bulldog was admitting to himself that he saw human life in a completely different way to how he'd ever seen it before. He was trying to explain to me that he had this weird feeling in his body, butterflies in his stomach. He was absolutely terrified that his emotional state would be visible to others. Bulldog needed information, skills and resources because in his words he was starting to think he actually cared. What he was doing was retrenching staff, something he'd always done and yet this time it was different.

Empathy is defined as the ability to appreciate or understand and share the feelings of another. It is different from sympathy which is to feel pity for someone's misfortune.

In life and in business, empathy is an important resource to have. It enables you to be authentic with yourself and others. With empathy you can safely express yourself without feeling vulnerable and needing to take on the role of rescuing others. Empathy also enables a stress release valve to be activated as internalising feelings can be uncomfortable and unhealthy. Having empathy also enables others to see your authentic self.

Empathy has its historical linguistic origins in ancient Greek. Psychologist Edward Titchener (1867-1927) introduced the term empathy into the English language. It was, however, Theodore Lipps (1851-1914) who was able to better articulate what Titchener had thought and was able to express how empathy was an internally evoked reaction. In the late 19th and early 20th Century, the term empathy was deemed to be the primary means of gaining knowledge into another person's mind. The theory was then almost neglected until many years later. In developing NLP in the 1970's, Bandler and Grinder created a list of presuppositions that are closely linked to looking at context and content in behaviours and to respecting another person's model of the world. They suggest people are not their behaviour and this enables a separation where instead of taking the reactions of another person personally you can instead use filters including empathy to see their reactions in context. Being able to appreciate what someone may be going through, particularly when you are making tough leadership decisions that impact them, is an important business skill which is often underrated.

Learning how to have empathy serve you in life and in business is an important aspect of being a great leader. To be effective I have some suggestions:

1. Use "I" language to own your words and your behaviour without deflecting. When you use "I" language you are effectively taking responsibility for your statements and this is really important in situations where you need the people you are communicating with to feel understood and to feel as though they are being respected. When you avoid "I" language what tends to happen is the person you are speaking to hears your words as blame or accusation as though they are somehow at fault.

2. Use "and" and avoid using "but" and "however." This is a really interesting language distinction when creating empathy

in conversation. The words "but" and "however" negate what was said directly before the conjunction. For example, "you look lovely today but your hair is out of place." What the non-conscious mind hears is, "you don't look lovely today because your hair is out of place." Same applies to however, "it's a lovely day however the winds are high." What the non-conscious hears is, "it's not a lovely day, it's windy." Rephrase these by replacing the "but" and "however" with "and" to achieve a completely different outcome. "You look lovely today and your hair is out of place." "It's a lovely day and the winds are high." When leading people and working to achieve outcomes in business I suggest you become very conscious of how and when to use "but" and "however."

3. Preface difficult conversations with the wording, "This may not land well and..." I often find giving someone a warning of what's about to be delivered in a conversation can help to reduce and even eliminate a negative response. One of my favourites is to use the words, "this may not land well..." One of the reasons for this is that the non-conscious mind misses negatives, so the word "not" in this statement may be missed. At the same time, you've alerted the person you are speaking to that what you are about to say may be unpleasant. Most people looking for upset or expecting upset will take the opposite line to you. In expressing before you make a statement that it may be unpalatable you effectively assist the conversation to be more positive. The person is less likely to be upset with you specifically if your delivery shows this level of empathy.

4. Repeat the other person's words back to them to gain empathy. For example, "a moment ago you said..." People want to be heard in difficult conversations and the best way for you to show respect and make this easy is to repeat words back to

them exactly as they have said them to you. I find this is especially effective when you want to show empathy because too many conversations become unnecessarily difficult when 1 person claims they want to be heard. The easiest and fastest way to prove you are listening is to repeat exact statements back to a person and then add onto these statements your own commentary to acknowledge them and move toward completion.

5. Appreciate that everyone has their own model of the world, beliefs, values and reactions. Their viewpoint is valid to them and needs nothing more than your respect.

6. When you want to point out to someone that they may be missing something, use the opening statement, "My story is telling me..." followed by, "can you help me to understand this?" Many behavioural theorists believe that as humans we struggle to be understood. When another person presupposes to understand, a gatekeeper rocks up and literally sets off a voice inside the head of the person receiving these words saying, "how could you understand me? You are you, not me!" By asking someone to "help you understand" you show an immense amount of empathy and advise the person you want to learn from them and hear them so you can treat them with respect.

What if you feel overwhelmed by empathy and think you are exposed to vulnerability as a result? See if a trusted friend or colleague can support you by giving you their viewpoint. Ask yourself the question, "how can I better support the outcome I want to achieve here?"

This was the day bulldog realised for the first time that he has empathy. He realised that understanding and appreciating another person's reaction is probably one of the most powerful gifts a leader can give anyone else. He told me that he realised everyone's life journey is about space and time. He felt happier than ever, more able to connect with people and found a new level of kindness in the people he needed to deliver difficult news to. The universe supports everyone's individual journey and even though he felt like the news he brought was all about loss, he was able to give many examples from his own life of opportunity disguised as loss. Through listening, he felt the effect of being grounded and empathetic and used his "I" words to own what he had to share.

When you take a new angle on the language skills of empathy you can change the way you lead, your happiness and the connections you keep in your world.

CHAPTER 15:
LIMITATIONS

"Every man takes the limits of his own field of vision for the limits of the world." ~ Arthur Schopenhauer

E very morning I go through my social media feeds to look for inspiring information and stories.

One Monday, I saw something interesting about bees and it made me think about limitations in business and leadership, more importantly how limitations inhibit success. What I found out is that the humble bumble bee is apparently aerodynamically unable to fly and they do anyway. The apparent explanation is fascinating.

Have you ever been told you could not do something and then proved the messenger wrong by doing it? People test these boundaries all the time. Starting in the playground as children and then accepting a dare as a teenager. Finding yourself injured or being labelled unintelligent, people step up to these challenges every day and prove something.

What is the proof? To me it's two things. Firstly, it's limitations and secondly its ownership.

Ever met someone who took on the opinion of another and owned it even though it stifled them and meant they lived half of who they really were? I went to school with a girl who was told she was fairly brainless and should pursue a career in home science. She took this on until years later someone else told her that they thought she was the exact opposite. So she went with this opinion and tested it out. Today, she is CEO of a large multi-national employing more than 500 people. Where do our beliefs about our limitations come from? Are they real?

Limitations are defined as shortcomings or defects. Ownership is defined as the act, state or right of possessing something. What are limitations and ownership really? They are a decision to operate within a boundary condition and to accept that condition as being the full extent of what is possible in that area of your life. Owning limitations can be helpful in keeping us safe and protected. They can also result in feelings of regret and a lack of meaningful fulfilment in your life.

In circumstances where limitations lead to frustration, apathy and regret, when you find ways to move past them it is rewarding and life changing. The result can be a renewed enthusiasm for life, breaking the boundaries of restrictions, spending time with people who inspire and motivate you and having a sense of self achievement in finding out more of who you really are.

The desire to understand the human mind dates back to Christian Wolff who first coined the concept and term psychology in the early 1700's. Later in the 1700's, Immanuel Kant suggested that rational mental processes must be activated by mental content derived from experience. Psychology in the 1970's found that neurological patterns were an essential factor in accessing the limitations that may be imposed by an individual on their own views of the world.

So if you wanted to, how could you elevate your experience from limitations? One way to do this is to find out what your goals are and then ascertain if you have any limiting beliefs that may prevent you from achieving what it is you want in your life.

In business and leadership, there are steps you can take to assess your vulnerability to limitations and to ascertain whether you are currently limiting yourself in areas of your life. I like to do this exercise with my mentoring clients to help them find out if they are living with limitations that are perhaps not serving them.

1.   When you were a child what recommendations were made to you about your future career?

2.   What beliefs did you grow up with around money and success from the adults most influential in your life? How have these shaped your beliefs about your capabilities?

3.   Looking back now, when you were young how were the adults most influential in your life living the life of their dreams? If they were not living the life of their dreams what did they say and do in relation to this belief?

4.   If you had no barriers to achievement and success how does what you are doing with your life right now compare with the life of your dreams or the life you'd prefer to be living?

5.   Who, if anyone, has inspired you by doing something with their life that you never thought possible for them?

6.   What barriers to success do you imagine are in your life right now? How could these be challenged and overcome?

7.   Answering these questions how do you rate your relationship with limitations? Are you living your deepest desired potential or are you holding yourself back?

What if you have some really significant limitations – perhaps health or physical which are very challenging? What you may want to consider is the road from here to your destination is not straight it's likely to have twists and many turns. It will possibly have unexpected setbacks and wins. You may even find that you achieve what it is you are seeking by some complete weird turn of events. To ask, "how could I" instead of, "why can't I" is perhaps the best check you could ever use.

The explanation for bumble bee flight with aerodynamic disadvantage is that the bee knows not that he cannot fly. Have you ever asked a blind person what's it like to be blind compared to seeing? It's probably one of the craziest questions you could ever ask. How do you know any different to what your normal is? To a blind person who functions in life and can do what a seeing man does, blindness is just a state, it's not a limitation.

CHAPTER 16:
CLARITY

"Whatever happens, take responsibility." ~ Tony Robbins

Feelings of confusion and uncertainty can be uncomfortable and that's why you may want to push through as quickly as possible. Yet you might want to hear how beneficial confusion and uncertainty can be in your life and how seeing the benefits may take you closer to living your dreams. In this chapter, I will share with you how confusion and uncertainty are simply the gateway to clarity and how these feelings are essential for progress and development in business and leadership.

One day, I was mentoring a professional who was confused about her career direction. The feelings stemmed from an experience she had just before the Global Financial Crisis (GFC). Everything was going well in her work in the banking and finance industry. Then, one day she received a call from a head-hunter who wanted to speak to her about an opportunity for career progression and promotion with a rival bank. She went through the process and after about 3 months of negotiation made the decision to leave the firm she'd been working at and after 15 years at this firm she moved to the rival. This decision cost her in terms of golden handcuffs and yet she was excited about the new role. Within 8 weeks at the new company, the GFC hit and less than 2.5 months after she'd joined, she was made redundant. It took her more than 12 months to find new employment. Her biggest issue was feelings of confusion and uncertainty in many areas of her life. They evoked emotional responses she knew were disproportionately high, yet the feeling in her body was so strong she couldn't help feeling overwhelmed. I knew this discussion would be transforming and that together we could find some solutions.

Confusion is a lack of clarity about what is intended, required or desired. In other words, it's a state of seeking, of answer finding and of creating new neural patterns to learn something for the first time. Uncertainty, from the word uncertain, is a state of hesitancy, instability, variability and subject to change.

Both confusion and uncertainty can be helpful from the point of view that they can help you move toward changes that can bring forth more of what you want in life. They provide an opportunity to learn and grow. These states can also help you move away from the mundane or activities, beliefs and behaviours that are not serving your higher purpose in life.

Throughout history confusion and uncertainty have been documented as part of a natural process of life. While it may be a little woo-woo for many people, the Tarot which was developed in the mid-15th century as a deck of 78 cards shows a process. One card in the pack, called the Moon card, signifies confusion, lack of clarity and worry. This card is directly followed by the Sun card which signifies optimism and enlightenment. In the Hero's Journey, American mythologist, writer and lecturer Joseph Campbell (1904-1987) describes the stages of growth involving trials, tests and upheavals which lead to self-mastery. A sense of accomplishment, freedom and reward comes from moving through times of confusion and uncertainty to the accelerated growth on the other side of this learning. The Hero's Journey reminds me of a quote from Winston Churchill that has always inspired me. Churchill's words were, "Success is not final, failure is not fatal: it is the courage to continue that counts." In the context of Campbell's Hero's Journey the process involves courage from the perspective that failure on the way is feedback and there isn't an end. The end of the journey is the beginning of the next at a new level of personal expansion and self-understanding.

So often, there is absolute gold in appreciating that confusion and uncertainty brings positive growth. It can bring immense growth for you in many areas of your life via a willingness to trust in the process, go through the trials and tribulations and find your aha moment. To be the hero of your journey is to see confusion and uncertainty as a gift.

In business and leadership, confusion and uncertainty is the frequent companion of entrepreneurs. What this means is that you are testing the boundaries of possibility and are prepared to step outside of your comfort zone in order to grow. All of these feelings are worth celebrating! Just like many people will proclaim it isn't easy to shed a few kilograms of bodyweight without some moments of hunger or run a marathon without some muscle pain. If you want to grow and excel as a leader in business, this will come with times of uncertainty and confusion. You are testing your limits and going into the new. Change means things will shift and evolve and new experiences you never considered before may show up in your life.

Here are four questions for self-inquiry when you are in a state of uncertainty and confusion:

1. There is no failure, only feedback. Become mindful of how you label confusion, delays and perceived hindrance in process. "What is the feedback here? What could I learn from this situation?"

2. Focus on what you want to find. Change all internal dialogue of, "Why can't I" instead to, "How could I?"

3. You are in charge of your mind and, therefore, your results. Focus on your own expansion by accepting yourself, and changing your behaviour. A great question to ask is, "What attitude do I most want to have in this situation for my own personal growth and happiness?"

4. Recognise that the person or system with the highest degree of flexibility of behaviour will control the system. Ask yourself, "how could I be even more flexible in my behaviour and attitudes."

All of these questions tap into the non-conscious part of your brain and deliver your outcomes. How the non-conscious mind works is that it stores memories, and represses all memories with an unresolved negative emotion. Your non-conscious mind takes everything personally and does not process negatives.

The professional I was mentoring found clear patterns of life experiences which left her with repressed negative emotions. This resulted in behaviour which was out of context and out of proportion in her life now. Being able to face this enabled her to find a new level of self-confidence and direction. She found new work that is even better than her previous circumstance and her career is on track again. Most importantly, she recognised the benefit of her periods of uncertainty in shaping the person she is today. She describes herself as more robust, insightful and with a higher degree of ingenuity in her work. She reads people and situations better and now knows the importance of ensuring her needs are met in ways that make her feel supported and safe. She believes none of this would have come into her consciousness without the uncertainty and confusion. This experience shaped her leadership and business life.

You may see similarities in your own life and be telling yourself - this sounds familiar. If this is you, then appreciating you are on a journey about growth will help you feel empowered knowing delays, trials and tribulations are part of the journey. No guts, no glory!

A phase of confusion and uncertainty in life can be likened to heavy rain followed by clear skies. The resolve to stay in process and experience the thresholds that are created in places of confusion and uncertainty can feel heroic and yet, what if this was exactly what has been designed to take your life journey to mastery in one area and/or another. No guts, no glory? Why does history repeat itself and ramp up a notch or two on the "this feels worse" scale when we put lessons aside? The answer may just be finding peace in a piece of confusion and uncertainty. In leadership and business, this is something worth embracing.

CHAPTER 17:
SEPARATING HEART FROM HEAD

"To handle yourself, use your head; to handle others, use your heart."
~ Eleanor Roosevelt

I t's a stomach churning feeling when your heart and head are in conflict. Not being sure whether to listen to either can leave you in a situation of no action or angst. How could you look at this from another angle? This happens often when you are in business and in your role as a leader. It can be a lonely place and the battle ground of internal conflict. In this chapter, I will give you some easy strategies for working out how to handle an issue of head and heart conflict.

I was reflecting on the importance of this one day when one of my executive clients contacted me in a state of distress. Big decisions on the table he asked me, "How do I separate my heart from my head?" My immediate reaction was intrigue because I had often experienced this myself, always managed to somehow resolve it and I was excited to help my client work through this knowing I was going to unpack a new strategy at the same time.

There was a long pause before we both laughed. He knew exactly what I was thinking. I was processing his suggestion literally and I had a very comical picture of a man in my mind's eye trying to pull his body apart. I said nothing and he immediately broke the silence by saying, "Come on Madelaine, I know what I am asking you is biological huri-kuri!" He was in pain from his feelings of upset over decisions that needed to be made.

My executive needed some resources to rationalise his feelings and I appreciated the fact. The resources we discussed assisted him to put the power of his heart and the power of his head together to achieve an unexpected resolution.

The heart is an organ that pumps oxygen-rich blood to every cell of your body. Your heartbeat is a muscle contraction that is vitally important for the quality of every cell. The head contains a number of very important parts including eyes to see, ears to hear, a mouth to eat, drink and make sounds from, and your head also contains your brain. Your brain sends life supporting messages to every cell of your body.

The benefits of bringing your heart and head together include reduced stress, fewer health problems including a reduction in stress induced headaches and palpitations. Oxygen rich blood flow works more efficiently to maximise energy. Clarity and energy increase happiness and confidence. Your capacity to be effective and harmonious in all areas of your life personally, with family and at work increases.

When someone wants to separate their heart from their head, what they are often really saying is, "how can I pull apart my emotional feelings from my analytical thinking? My analytical thinking is making me feel heartless and my emotional feelings are making me feel incompetent."

What would be immensely beneficial for the individual is to do the exact opposite.

I find the conflict of heart and head stems back to the separation of two parts within the psyche that were once part of a greater whole. What the heart and head want can often be the same outcome, however the neurological pathway to realising this has become disconnected. Actually re-connecting pathways in the brain and finding out what the head (thinking, rational, strategic) wants and the heart (emotional, life giving, vulnerable) wants can bring about a reduction in internal conflict.

Clarity and power comes from asking yourself, "Heart and head, how could you work together right now to achieve an outcome that goes beyond my expectation and produce something incredible in this situation?" In a moment of internal conflict, this is how you could break the boundaries to expand your thinking.

So with my client, I wanted to find the disconnect points which I suspected were once part of a greater whole.

These are the steps to the solution:

- Take a piece of paper, a pen and created 2 columns. On one side "head" and the other side "heart."

- Write down all the thoughts that come into your mind asking yourself, "What does my heart say?" And then "What does my head say?" Allocate the responses to each column. Some will end up in both columns.

- When this feels complete have a look at the list and number each item in the columns by importance to you, so your most important "head" response will be number one and so on. Do the same for your "head" column.

- Then turn the piece of paper over and write down the outcome that you are looking for from the conflict situation.

You are writing the outcome instead of the process here. The outcome you are looking for will be something you really want to achieve. This may be outstanding team performance, profit achieved, we have the best clients in the world, all our clients love us, we achieve amazing results, I achieve all my goals with ease etc.

- Go back to your columns and look at your top 6 "head" and "heart" thoughts about the issue in each column. Ask yourself, "Does this absolutely help me achieve my outcome?" Mark next to the item yes or no.

- Take the "yes" items for each list and collate them on a separate piece of paper.

- Integrate these and then act on these items as they are your top priorities for achieving your outcome and these have been determined from your combined list of using your head and your heart.

What if you still have an issue with separating heart from head? It can be helpful to ask a trusted friend or colleague to help you break the boundaries and look for an integrated solution. Instead of asking them to help you separate heart from head, ask them the opposite. Ask them, "How could I bring my heart and head together?"

My executive client did not perform huri-kuri! We did have a good laugh though. He was able to find a solution to his problem that ultimately turned out to be highly beneficial for all parties. What he found most remarkable was how he felt making the decision. He describes the congruency as life changing. For the first time in many years, he described a combined feeling of immense pride, love, compassion and solid business sensibility. He received verbal feedback and appreciation from his colleagues which he had never received before. He truly saw himself as a competent leader.

To see the benefits you gain from having your heart and head work together can be life changing. You just need to tell yourself a different story. A feeling of congruency, power, love, intelligence and pride in decisions is your gift for the effort.

CHAPTER 18:
A QUANTUM LEAP AT THE CENTRE OF YOUR UNIVERSE

"You can search throughout the entire universe for someone who is more deserving of your love and affection than you are yourself, and that person is not to be found anywhere. You yourself, as much as anybody in the entire universe deserve your love and affection." ~ Buddha

I s it your time to stop the endless search? Is it your time to decide that you are the centre of your universe and you choose to live your life this way from today? In leadership and business giving is so important to your success and your ability to take others on a journey of life change. This is what a leader does. They keep their energy vibration at the highest level possible and then inspire and take others on a journey. In this chapter, I share the gift of discovering what really matters to you and show you how to integrate it into your life.

The world is not going to slow down and wait for you. What if you didn't even need it to slow down and wait for you? Imagine being able to set the pace of your own life and create a plan for the year ahead that sees you firmly placed at the centre of your own universe. Selfish or self-full? There is no one in this world like you. There is no one else more deserving of your own love and self-focus than you are.

So what happens in leadership and entrepreneurship when everything and everyone feels draining? This can happen and you'll hear people referring to it as burnout. The challenge is that circumstances are unlikely to change unless you as the leader change.

A number of years ago, I was working with a physiotherapist and one day we had a discussion about breaking the boundaries of self-imposed limitations. By this I was referring to the limiting decisions some people make that keep them from living the life of their dreams. I realised that one of the most significant deciding factors in achieving a level of self-potential was the decision on whether to be the centre of your own universe or to relinquish this to others. Working with my client, I decided to show her how to become the centre of her own universe.

First we discussed some definitions, so we had some scope on what we were approaching. A quantum leap is a sudden and highly significant advance or breakthrough. The universe is all existing matter and space considered as a whole. It is also the realm in which something exists. Approaching your life in this way means making some new choices that will impact all areas of your life in ways that serve you. Some people avoid this, feeling it's a narcissistic way of living. Narcissism involves having an overwhelming need and craving for admiration from others. The purpose of being the centre of your own universe is for you to live your highest individual ideals in life independent of the approval of others. When you have a universal approach, start with a tonne of goodness for yourself and then expand this out to everyone around you.

There is little more generous and life supporting than doing this for yourself and others.

Why be the centre of your own universe in life, business and leadership? Being the centre of your own universe can be helpful in all areas of your life. At work, it helps you to be assertive, know your direction and not take on other people's problems as your own. It helps you to achieve your goals and be calm and measured. In relationships, it helps you to be positive, self-assured and to have an aura of confidence. It enables you to give without expectations and to receive without strings. It also helps you to fill the gaps by giving to yourself whenever you need to without any guilt. In health, it helps you to look after your wellbeing and be accountable for your choices. In leadership and business, it allows you to have clarity for your own direction and responsibilities and limit the possibility of being clouded by the demands of others. Rather than being enmeshed and intertwined with the needs of others, it allows you to work in parallel and alongside other people where everyone is free to be successful and stand in their own light.

So how do you make yourself the centre of your own universe? You need a strategy and some techniques. There are 5 steps.

1. Make a list of all of the things you like, the things that make you happy and the things that are really important to you. Make sure that everything on this list relies on you and you alone. It needs to be all about you. Not about others or what others do for you. With this list choose your top ten not negotiable items.

2. With your top 10 in place. Consider how many of these priority items you are currently giving yourself every day. If there are items on the list that you have as a desired outcome and are not experiencing right now highlight these.

3. Next ask yourself what you could do on a daily, weekly,

monthly or annual basis to move toward achieving the items you currently want in your life, which are evading you. Remember this is about being the centre of your own universe, so if someone else is preventing you, you need to be accountable for finding an avenue around this hurdle. This is about what you need to do for yourself, not what others need to do for you. Being the centre of your own universe means being at cause and take responsibility for your own outcomes.

4. Brainstorm all the ideas that you could adopt to have more of what you want in your life. More of what will place you at the centre of your own universe. Then simplify your actions to enable easy repetition or duplication.

5. Take out your diary or year planner and fill in the activities you commit to doing to be the centre of your own universe. Remember it's about small steps and big rewards.

What if you find that you are way off target from living at the centre of your own universe? Speak to a trusted friend who may be able to give you some ideas on how you could move toward more of what you want in life. Make sure you choose a friend who is positive, caring and who has achieved more of what you want. You could also look at doing some personal development work and this can be accessed through community, internet and short courses.

Not a day passes without me giving someone the gift of my two ears to hear about how they hope to have the life of their dreams one day. What I hear about are the limitations and obstacles, the generalisations and deletions that make someone feel better and maybe help them edge toward what they want. A generalisation in this context refers to the deliberate oversimplification of an experience to reduce emotional impact and deletion in this context refers to leaving information out as a means to comfort the impact of missing out on something you have longed for. This doesn't need to be so. As the centre of your universe, what matters is you and in that all perfect in the moment you. How does your life look now when you deliberately take small frequent steps to make yourself the centre of your own universe? Knowing what is important to you will help you find the balance and enable you to have even more energy in your leadership roles.

"Most people overestimate what they can do in one
year and underestimate what they can do in ten years."
Bill Gates

CHAPTER 19:
LOOKING FOR 2%

"So you're a little weird? Work it! A little different OWN it! Better to be a nerd than one of the herd!" ~ Mandy Hale

The feeling I have is pretty special when I am at collaborative round table meetings with influential people about influencing changes. I hear lots of great ideas and enthusiasm around the table and yet what I so often see is a painfully slow, if any, execution of the great ideas being shared. Entrepreneurial business success relies on your ability to listen carefully and be a part of round table discussions, and then to know when your own initiative needs to kick in to get out of talk mode and actually get things moving.

At the end of the meetings with committees, I tend to cringe if the host goes around the table for a parting comment from each delegate as I'm always afraid that what I will share may not land well. I'm impatient and I like to see progress. I'm the first to admit that I'm embarrassed at the number of "positive change meetings" I go to that result in zero change. These days I look for the 2% just in case the group doesn't get it together.

In this chapter, I share with you what only 2% of people are willing to do. This is so important for business and leadership. It's the "difference" that makes the difference.

Let me tell you about the 2%.

One day in 1939, a man by the name of Nicholas Winton, a London stockbroker aged just 29 went on a ski holiday to Switzerland and visited a friend in Prague on the way. He sensed the danger in Nazi Germany and he became impatient. He could not wait for "action by committee" so he did what most people would consider impossible. He worked from his hotel room and made arrangements that saved 669 children from Nazi Germany. Needing a special British visa for each child he advertised and sought sponsorship from British families who were at the time allowed to sponsor one person. Every visa saved one child. He arranged and paid for special trains to move the children from certain death in Germany to safety in Britain. He then went back to his daily life making no mention of his initiative.

The 2% are those who live amongst the 98% of people who say no, and the 98% who need management by committee to be effective. The 2% are defined by helping other people in innovative ways, when everyone else either says it cannot be done or is otherwise fussing, waiting for the committee to agree and still trying to get organised.

Our world needs to grow the 2% to effect change and to help lead a massive result of actions that create a better life for others. You create greatness, save lives and enable other people to live in much better circumstances when you actually do what 98% of people cannot or won't do. You can literally save lives and change generations.

Historically, we have many examples of people who, just like Winton, have taken initiative to change the lives of others by taking action quickly, and without a committee. Some, of course, are incredibly famous like Nelson Mandela (1918-2013) and Martin Luther King (1929-1968). Then there are people like Australians Bruce and Denise Morcombe who set up a foundation and became educators teaching children about personal safety. Patricia Mowbray in the Australian Capital Territory who was unable to have biological children so instead decided to adopt special needs children. She has three Down Syndrome children and devotes her time to the care and education of special needs children in her city. And there are people who simply see what needs to be done and volunteer because they can. They are all in the 2%.

To become part of the 2% is actually easier than most people think. You could start right now in what may seem like the smallest ways, and create life changing results. After the meetings I go to, I deliberately step out and effect change as instantly as I can. And this is how I do it:

1. **Random acts of kindness.** Find someone at the train station begging for a dollar because that's all their self-esteem tells them they're worth and give them $50 because you know they are worth more even if you think they will spend it on something harmful.

2. **Dare yourself to keep sharing** your craziest change for the greater good ideas with 98 people until you find the last 2 who will believe, support and encourage you without rubbishing your apparent nuttiness behind your back.

3. **Mentor someone in your office** who would least expect the encouragement and esteem your care and attention will give them.

4. **Treat the world as the round place** that it is. Continually pay it forward by helping in areas where you can, because you know that what goes around comes around.

5. **Be the leader** and when you bring a committee together

empower the follow through to make it happen and if it's falling apart, have the courage to go it alone without concern for egos.

So what if this just doesn't happen on such a grand scale and you know in your heart you are in the 2%? Turn to the person behind you in the supermarket queue, smile, say something and make their day. You never know the impact a smile can have. Or take the time to look someone you really care about in the eye in a staring contest that allows you to see their soul. This is actually leadership. And if you are unsure about your own soul then have a staring contest with a mirror. You might just see such beauty that it makes you cry. 98% of people never do this. You can do something good every day that 98% of people would never do.

After Nicholas Winton saved 669 children and continued his ordinary life he was so humble that he told no one of his actions, not even Grete the woman he later married. One day in 1988, Grete was cleaning up and going through some boxes and she found a scrap book with a catalogue of records on the children from 1939. Soon after this time, Winton was in the audience at the filming of what he thought was a documentary on holocaust survivors and he was surprised to find the person sitting next to him had arrived on one of the trains. The broadcast host soon asked if anyone in the audience had arrived in Britain as a child on one of the trains and two dozen people stood up. Winton had been coaxed under false pretences and the documentary was actually an episode of "This is your Life" in his honour. His actions saved not only the 669 children, in 2009, their descendants amounted to more than 5,000 people.

To see life through the eyes of someone who operates from the 2% is humbling, special and incredibly inspiring. And yet all we each need to do is to tell ourselves that we are the change we want to see in the world. If you are telling yourself that you love the committee and are itching for the action then start in the smallest of ways to lead and feel what it feels like to do what 98% of people would never do.

CHAPTER 20:
PRO-BONO. WHO ARE YOU KIDDING?

"Dare to love yourself as if you were a rainbow with gold at both ends."
~The River of Winged Dreams

The definition of pro-bono is to undertake a task without compensation for the good of the public. Highly successful professionals who undertake pro-bono work are at the heart of helping people at times when the need is high and ability to afford such qualified services is low. This is honourable and special. When new industry professionals and new business leaders looking for work offer pro-bono services there's a problem. Is this called pro-bono or is this called amateur? Amateur to me in this context is un-skilled or inexperienced and offering free services as a way to enter a profession, and it's very different to pro-bono. If you have ever done this you need a better solution.

In this chapter, I give you the steps to resolve the issue of free work disguised as pro-bono. I will also show you how to effectively and easily increase your prices as you progress in business.

The problem many new professionals and new business owners face is establishing clientele and a sound reputation. A solution often considered is to offer services free of charge in the hope that this will translate to either a client or referral to potential clients. Because the outcome the professional or entrepreneur is looking for is real clients and a good reputation, they offer free services to clients who can afford to pay. Time and time again I have met incredibly talented professionals and entrepreneurs who struggle in business because they are a doormat of free services. They provide so much "pro-bono" work they are literally starving while suiting up to look professional and pretend all is okay for their so called clients. This is not pro-bono, this is amateur.

In February 2013, Dunn and Bradstreet reported that small business failures in 2011 had risen by 48%. The largest impact was cash flow, with a knock on effect impacting other businesses. More than 60% of businesses are receiving payments after 30 days. The key message being touted is for small businesses to mitigate their cash flow risk. This would seem impossible if starting your business has been on the platform of free services. Perhaps another issue is at play, and is often a factor I identify when working with new professionals. It comes down to self-esteem and internal challenges about self-worth and ability. I find myself quoting the words of the late US Psychiatrist, M Scott Peck, "Until you value yourself, you won't value your time. Until you value your time, you will not do anything with it. "

The pro-bono test is a simple one. If you are a business person who currently earns at a high level, who has a wealth of years in business, who receives lots of referrals, who earns from every action, who charges at the higher end in your industry and one day you are asked to help someone who cannot otherwise afford your services and the impact of giving them free advice is less than a 1% on your bottom line then it's called pro-bono. Go for it. If, however, you are new to business, strug-gling, or trying to establish yourself and your reputation, and you offer your services for free, this is called a business problem and you need a solution.

1. Be really clear on what your services are and what price you set for each service. Making sure you are congruent with this is a self-worth and self-esteem question. If you cannot give someone a 30-second elevator speech on what you do and how you charge then it's not going to be easy for a client to engage your services or products. This applies if you have your own business or are a leader in someone else's business. Know your product, your services and your fees.

2. Decide who your ideal client is and write it down so you can specifically and categorically pick them out in a sea of people and set yourself up for success. Describe who they are, what they need, how you help them and what the exchange is. If you are in business, it's an exchange of services or goods for money. Be clear on this. If you are a leader working in an organisation you are responsible for budgets, so the criteria and process is the same as for someone in free enterprise.

3. If you are in your own business and want to grow or are newly established and want to create the steps to achieve your ideal exchange of services for fees, how do you set a price and get started? With many professionals, I suggest they take steps to test the market. I also follow this strategy with the health professionals I mentor. It's okay to start your first client low, the next one you step up a little, then the next a little more. Or you set thresholds, choose a price for the first 10 hours or first 10 clients and then step up from there. As soon as your time fills, you increase again for new clients. You'll soon find your equilibrium level. This level is where you

are maintaining hours or clients and demand is slowing. You're busy. If you are a leader working in an organisation make sure you use all the resources of the company to give your clients the highest value for money. Sometimes leaders who are in charge of revenue generation do too much themselves and fail to draw on staff and services within the company to create leverage to enhance the client experience.

4. Every year, take an inflation price rise, even $1. This way you start as you intend to progress, as a business person, exchanging services for fees. Look at ways to add even more value. Re-promote what you do every year. Take it to the next level. At the start of every year, send a letter to all of your clients letting them know what's happening in your world, inspire them and give them information about your services. Always tell them you are a referral based business. Naturally, if you have a client that you never want to deal with again, delete them from your list!

5. Then when you are basking in your professional glory, established and with a fine reputation, you can offer pro-bono services to someone who truly cannot afford you and needs your help.

Here are two warning lights to be aware of. The first being what if business takes off really slowly and you are at your lowest price too long? Well, you are still in a much better place than free "door matting" yourself. Look at ways to add services and upsell the clients you have or change your offer to suit a wider market. The second warning light is the problem of getting really busy fast and not increasing your price fast enough. Create scarcity by being aware of your thresholds and stick to them.

CHAPTER 21:
EATING AN ELEPHANT

"A goal without a date is just a dream." ~ Milton Erickson

In this chapter, I share with you my experience with learning from and modelling the successes of a business leader I have seen create an amazing empire. I caught up with a very successful businessman and dear friend when by chance we happened to be in transit through the same city on the same day. He started his global empire on his own about 15 years ago. His business is dynamic, a global leader and very large. It employs thousands of people across 4 continents and is leading his industry in innovation, delivery and customer service.

I knew this man 15 years ago when he was talking about the dream of starting this venture. At the time, he told me of his plans and goals. Jokingly I told him I hoped it would not become a white elephant. The origin of the phrase white elephant apparently dates back to the 17th century in Asia. If you owned an albino elephant it was not very useful and needed to be fed special food. The white elephant was also considered to have some spiritual qualities so if you owned one, it was essential that you made it available for people to visit and pray to. Basically, it cost a fortune to keep, took up all of your time and was otherwise useless. When I laughed with my friend about his business venture 15 years ago, I was actually saying to him that it sounded like more trouble than it was worth, hence the white elephant comment.

My white elephant comment did not fall on deaf ears. He asked me at the time, "Do you know how to eat an elephant?" I must have squirmed as I had this gross visual of chewing some tough indigestible BBQ. He said to me, "one bite at a time." I'm pretty sure we both laughed at this point about how gross that would be, but, the symbolism of this discussion on reflection is not a joke at all.

My friend knew his project was elephant sized. He also knew that he was taking on something that most people would think was a burden, like a white elephant. He also knew that to tackle all of his huge ideas, he needed to break the steps down to reach his goals into the smallest steps possible to ensure he could see progress and have others work successfully with him, like eating an elephant one bite at a time. This is exactly what he did.

Goals are great, but, without a step by step plan that measures and celebrates along the way they are useless and not worth more than a dream. Harvard University once surveyed their MBA students and found that 83% had no goals, 13% had goals but they were not in writing, and 3% had clearly defined their goals and written them down. Apparently 10 years later the same group was surveyed and the 3% that had clear, documented goals were earning on average 10 times the average income of the other 97%.

In large projects, leveraging time and resources is an important aspect of business and leadership success. "Leveraging" means using something to maximum advantage and applying a smaller amount of exertion to

achieve a multiplied result. In leadership and business, when you learn how to use this to your advantage you save time and money. Taking on a big project also means having the foresight to appreciate there are going to be much better skilled resources than you can offer in certain aspects of the project. The best leaders in business surround themselves with people who have highly specialised specific skills the leader him or herself does not have. This is a key to growing your leadership and success which small business people, consultants and managers can apply to reap enormous benefit.

As a business leader or entrepreneur here are the effective steps to breaking down your elephant sized project into small bites:

1. Start with a few big pieces of cardboard, pens and a few pads of sticky notes.

2. On the large pieces of cardboard write headings of the major outcomes you want to achieve in the business.

3. On the sticky notes start writing all the small tasks that need to be done.

4. Place the sticky notes with small tasks onto the poster that best fits the outcome that small task will support once completed.

5. Go to each poster and re-look at all the sticky notes to make sure they are aligned and will definitely be essential for the final outcome. Peel off anything that is a task for task sake that will not make a positive or negative difference. Throw these in the bin. Add onto the poster any extra sticky notes of tasks that you've missed.

6. Now look at each poster and the tasks and move the sticky notes around to group them in the best way to get them done while leveraging time, expertise and resources. You can have

sub-contractors and consultants complete some of the tasks now that you have a clear idea of what needs to be done.

7. Make a plan for each task, bring in the resources needed. Put a big smiley face on each sticky note as the tasks are completed. In the end, you will be seeing incredible progress, you'll know what's outstanding at a glance and you'll have dozens of smiley's rewarding you for great planning and awesome execution.

For every big elephant sized idea he had, my friend decided on the outcome, strategy and every step needed to complete it. He celebrated the small stuff and found his big lofty dreams floated toward him without him even realising sometimes how incredibly well things were coming together. He simplified and multiplied. When small steps did not work, course correction was relatively easy. Rework was minimised by a small step approach and measurement. He also celebrates tackling something that others thought would be more trouble than it was worth.

Could this approach be the missing link in the "one day" dreams you have in your business and leadership? The ability to form your own perception and break free of the invisible limitation posed by the perceptions of yourself and others gives you the chance to look at the entire project. This is easy to do and easy not to do. I've never seen more compelling evidence of just how this process can transform lives as I have in the case of my friend.

CHAPTER 22:
BEING FOLLOWED BY IDIOTS

"To every rule there is an exception—and an idiot ready to
demonstrate it. Don't be the one!" ~ Vera Nazarian

In this chapter, I share something so simple and yet so profound
that if you as a business person and leader can master it with
self-evaluation and self-awareness has the power to transform
everything in your world. Blockages to success will lift. Your
ability to hear people and read them accurately will be enhanced.
More importantly than anything, your ability to understand your
influence and involvement in what irritates and annoys you in other
people can be managed and eliminated for good.

I want to share the story of one of my mentoring clients.

One day she called me and was panicked. She said it was super urgent.
She needed to speak to me ASAP. I was highly curious and wanted to

see what was going on, although I had my suspicions that I knew what the call was all about.

To preserve the reputation of this gorgeous woman who has experienced one of the biggest "ah-ha" moments in her life, I'm going to call her Lisa, not her real name.

Lisa had recently started a new job in the financial services sector. This was her 4th move in 5 years so her resume was starting to look a little patchy. Her biggest concern this time which prompted the move was she had become impatient with all the "idiots" she was working with.

So I get the call... It's 3 weeks into her new role and we have a mentoring session planned for a few weeks down the track. It's urgent. I call her back and a deflated and anxious Lisa says, "Why are all the people I work with idiots who don't get it?"

Okay this will be interesting. This is her 4th move in 5 years, so the only constant here is Lisa. The company, geography, corporate culture and the people are yet again different. How might it be possible that Lisa has once again stumbled on her arch nemesis in the workplace... "the idiot."

Lisa wanted to be an effective leader and yet she was finding the same problems following her into new environments.

In Neuro Linguistic Programming there is a concept known as, "perception is projection." In the prime directives of the unconscious mind what this basically suggests is that what you see in others is a reflection of yourself. It can be a very helpful understanding to have when the same issues crop up in relationships with different people and when there are rule violations in your dealings with others that lead you to believe you are right and they are wrong.

What this concept allows for is to find a deeper understanding of your personal role in the experiences you are having with others on a daily basis. Appreciating what you notice in others by reflecting this on what you are not seeing about yourself is a way to gain personal freedom, reduce your stress levels, get along with people more harmoniously, develop a mental toughness and be kinder to yourself and others.

I refer to perception is projection as personal behaviour blindness. One of the simplest ways to experience your personal behavioural blindness, which everyone has, is to notice what you see in others and what your judgements and perceptions are. This is especially telling on experiences that trigger you emotionally and for want of another term "press your buttons."

There are 4 steps to identifying and then creating a better outcome when it comes to ongoing issues with repeated events, situations and people that trigger you.

1. Pretend you are watching the situation or event that created the trigger as a movie replay. Imagine you are sitting in a movie theatre and up on the screen you can see yourself, the other people involved and the situation unfold. Get this really clear like you are watching a replay.

2. Write down all of the things the other people are doing in the movie that trigger, annoy you, make you think they are idiots, prevent you from getting your outcomes achieved and make you feel upset or angry.

3. Look at the list of triggers and ask yourself, "Where in my life do I do this same behaviour?" Be really honest and look carefully at where what has upset you is a mirror of what you also do.

4. When you've worked out what you do that is similar you have your trigger. The key now is for you to ask yourself, "How could I do things differently?" Change your actions that are

similar, even if they are in a completely different area of your life. By doing this, you will set up the opportunity to change your reality in your relationships with others. Changing another person isn't easy at all, and the best example I have to give you is to reflect on what it truly takes to change yourself. The gift in step 4 is that when you change your actions, no matter what unrelated area of life they are in, everything changes in all areas of your life.

To take these steps requires a willingness to look kindly and honestly at yourself as the sorts of reflections you are likely to see are things you'll find ugly and annoying. Instead of labelling these observations as good or bad, ask a better question like, "How could I use this reflection to bring out the best of who I really am?" What you see in others is often a reflection of you. Have you ever heard someone say, "No judgement, but...." Okay, That's going to sound like judgement!

What if this becomes overwhelming or you get a fright when you see your own shadow? The biggest gift you can give yourself is self-compassion and empathy. Just recognising the reflection will go a massive distance toward appreciating even more the behaviour that serves you. Above all you are not your behaviour and you can change your behaviour in a heartbeat. Speak to someone who cares to listen and if needed find a mentor or coach.

Since this discovery Lisa has transformed and is happier and more confident than she's ever given herself the freedom to be in the past. Her work situation is reflecting this shift and she's never felt more liked and more productive in her entire career.

Lisa saw the "idiot" in other people and this was frustrating and annoying to her. Learning about her own perception as a projection was a moment of freedom for Lisa. All of her life she had continually moved on – in jobs, relationships, even where she lived hoping to find people that she felt understood her. Lisa has discovered that she first needs to understand, and then be understood. The first person Lisa needed to understand was herself.

CHAPTER 23:
DOING INDISPENSABLE WHEN YOU SEEK APPRECIATION

"There is something beautiful in you seeking freedom." ~ Bryant McGill

I have a feeling that confusion between appreciation and being indispensable occurs in many disguised ways. I've heard it often, and when the cycle of finding the source has been found the vision is the same. Doing indispensable when what you seek is appreciation could be commonplace. In this chapter, I show you the important distinction in business and leadership that separates behaviours which fall short of making you feel appreciated.

I was working with a group of executives once and found an interesting blend of cross-contaminating behaviours. I was called in to assist with a productivity issue. My aim was first to seek to understand and then to be understood. These workshops are often the most fascinating and transforming as the group goes through a hero's journey of transformation. As we hit our first threshold in the discussion I saw the group heading for the dark night of the soul. On one side, I had a group of managers seeking appreciation, and yet their behaviour was driven by actions that they hoped would make them indispensable. On the other side, I had a group of managers oblivious to the efforts of the group who were rotating between wanting to be appreciated with their behaviour mixed up in talk of being indispensable. By the third example, it had to be surfaced.

Let me explain how this unfolded.

First manager says, "I intuit what will make it impossible for my manager to second guess my abilities, and this is what I do in my job." Second manager says, "I do the tasks that I know no one else can do as well as I do because I want to feel secure." Third manager said, "I hope my boss thinks I am indispensable."

What was so interesting about each of these statements was that it was obvious each person was feeling overwhelmed by wanting to have a high level of security. This was possibly leading to over thinking and what I observed was stress and exhaustion. Does this sound familiar or do you know someone who is just like this? I needed some resources and thankfully found some surprising answers.

Indispensable is defined as absolutely necessary and essential. Appreciation is defined as recognising the value, and full worth of something or someone. That these two attributes became enmeshed in a working environment is both interesting and revealing.

Why would you want to be indispensable? Well, what I found with this group was that the main reasons were for job security and fear of loss. The group shared situations, feelings and conditions that they wanted to move away from. This is how it plays out in large businesses with paid executives. In smaller businesses and with consultants, I see this becoming an issue when an entrepreneur moves away from their core and tries to please everyone. They take on tasks that are not their skill or they redefine how they do things to fit in with their client. They end up providing different things to everyone they deal with because they have stepped out of leadership in what they do. The ultimate cost is high due to changes in direction, a lack of relevance, inability to leverage services, and challenges with delegating work to other people because each client has completely different special needs totally outside the business framework. Resulting in long, unrewarding hours and in the end stress and overwhelm.

When asking why someone would want to be appreciated I found many more exciting reasons like job satisfaction, to feel good, to feel worthwhile, to have confidence, it makes me feel healthier, when I know where I stand I feel great, and I'm motivated to be a leader. The same applies to business owners. When a business owner feels appreciated the self-confidence this brings is energising and it inspires you to expand and grow.

In the group session, I needed to discover what was going on within the organisation and management team that had led to the indispensable verses appreciated equation. Historically, I found the organisation rewarded the very behaviours that were stressing staff out.

The company had been through many redundancies and changes in management and role responsibilities since the Global Financial Crisis. What's interesting is that on 17 January 2014, News Limited reported that the GFC "killed" 250,000 jobs in Australia. Given that in January 2014, the labour force in Australia, as reported by the Australian Bureau of Statistics, was 11,459,000 this means that each employed person had a one in 45 chance of losing his or her job. For every 45 white collar contacts on LinkedIn, chances are one person was a GFC job loss victim. In some industries like Banking and Finance where I just happened to be working when this issue came up the statistics were much higher.

How is it possible to turn this around? The team here were expressing that their stress was dire and their work performance was being driven by survival and not by the values, ethics and attitudes they knew would result in a much more productive, fun and harmonious work environment?

What I find works well for shifting this issue is to use a process of personal values elicitation, followed by creating your values hierarchy.

Here are the steps to find out your personal values and then decide what conditions you need to feel appreciated:

1. Take 7 pieces of paper and some pens.

2. On the top of each page write a title. These are Career on page 1, Family on page 2, Relationships on page 3, Personal Growth on page 4, Health / Fitness on page 5, Spirituality on page 6 and Lifestyle on page 7.

3. Start with page 1 and finish with page 7. Ask yourself, "What is important to me about....?" So for example, on page 1 you'll be writing a list of everything that's important to you about your career. List everything you can think of.

4. Next, go back to each sheet and number your top 10 values in each category.

5. Now that you have your top 10 in each category, get another piece of paper and create 7 columns. Head the columns with the area of your life and in order list your top 10 values for each section.

6. Look for the similarities and the differences. Then ask yourself while observing your values, "What do I need to feel appreciated?" Write it down starting the statement with, "I

appreciate being..." For example, your statement may say something like this, "I appreciate being loved, heard, supported, financially rewarded..."

7. Reflect on the actions you take to be indispensable when you are actually seeking appreciation and ask yourself, "Who am I and what do I do when I am appreciated." Write it down and action it.

Look objectively at this and own it. This is the very best of who you are. Have the courage to share your discovery with colleagues and trusted mentors who will assist you in changing attitudes in your business or work environment. A moment of powerful realisation hits when people see the commonality of their values.

Of course, there can be aspects of being so direct with a group which can create a sense that this process may not be easy. There are people who will shy away from revealing what they really feel and this is normal. You need to support and honour the individual.

The moment of transformation in this group was revealed when they realised that the simplicity of appreciation was being wound up in a game of trying to be indispensable. Evaluating the personal cost of this was ground-breaking. No one deserves to be stressed to the point of acting out in ways that are not character defining just in order to protect their employment. This group realised was just how this was bringing out the worst and not the best in the group. With this realisation now in place and with careful management and training strategies that support individual performance and job satisfaction, I look forward to seeing this group fly. They now tell themselves they can. What's even better, they created the feeling by their courage and willingness to face something quite unusual.

CHAPTER 24:
SAY GOODBYE TO PROCRASTINATION

"The really happy people are those who have broken the chains of procrastination, those who find satisfaction in doing the job at hand. They're full of eagerness, zest, productivity. You can be, too." ~ Norman Vincent Peale

There are times when you feel like a fresh start. It's easy to hear this self-talk and to set some new resolutions and then watch the months go by with little change. It's painful to have resolutions set and not achieved and it's great to have ambition and new goals to achieve. So how can you move just one thing out of the way and make this your time to truly achieve the things that mean so much to you? It's time to say goodbye to procrastination and in this chapter I explain what procrastination really might be and how to get the results you are looking for.

Some time ago, I had a business owner come to me for mentoring. He was exhausted and over the rat race. He described his life as a state of heightened alert, looking for the next problem to extinguish and so busy being on high alert and needing to "fire fight" that he achieved none of what he really wanted. He said it felt like he was procrastinating on the important and non-urgent projects, and was too exhausted dealing with daily reactive behaviour in most areas of his life meaning he had little of what he really wanted. He described wasting energy on keeping apparent imminent threats at bay, most of which resulted in nothing except wasting his time. We decided to look closely at what procrastination really is to help him move out of this place.

What is procrastination? The textbook definition is: to put off doing something, especially out of habitual carelessness or laziness; to postpone or delay needlessly. What is procrastination really? What I see with people who procrastinate is they feel they are under siege by opportunities and tasks. The flip side of procrastination is to focus, and take massive action; to seize something swiftly and eagerly. A person who is exhausted from trying to put out proverbial small fires all day has no energy to focus, take massive action or seize anything swiftly.

Being on high alert has its benefits, including a fast response to danger and keeping issues at bay. What this also does is prevents important, non-urgent projects and goals being achieved. The downside is exhaustion. Adrenal energy when used over long periods of time can have negative health implications. Life is not meant to be lived in an over functioning state of high alert. This is the state that prevents meaningful progress of important non-urgent activities. As technology advances, we have even more distractions and situations that cause a heightened state of alert that prevents progress on important tasks. So switching to actions that are about seizing the day, acting swiftly and focussing intently without distraction create progress which leads to happiness. This behaviour of progress also allows times of rest to gather energy, ready for the massive action that is needed to seize swiftly. This helps us to feel energised, refreshed, purposeful, truly effective and a leader.

The identification of procrastination dates back to the 17th Century and a sermon by a clergyman named Reverend Walker who refers to procrastination in the context of avoidance and delay. Abraham Lincoln is famously quoted saying, "you cannot escape the responsibility of tomorrow by evading it today."

How can you switch from the behaviour of being under siege and needing to react continually to being able to rest, focus and then swiftly act on the important tasks?

A great start is to look at the opposite of procrastination. To me the opposite of procrastination is anticipation. Look ahead and take action beforehand. I have used this in my business for over 20 years and it is by far one of the most critical things an entrepreneur and business leader can master. In my business, I currently employ 15 people and anticipating staff recruitment needs ahead of time has always been a fundamental factor in my planning and work. I anticipate market share, advertising needs and regulatory changes. I read business sentiment to anticipate how this may impact consumer behaviour. Working from a viewpoint of anticipation is an essential requirement in leadership.

To flip from procrastination to anticipation isn't always easy and yet there are some action steps that can be taken to break the cycle of reactive management which leads to no action at all.

I suggest the following action steps:

1. Start by looking at all the activities you feel need your immediate attention and make you feel under siege, as "options" and "opportunities."

2. Take the pressure off and instead of feeling overwhelmed by them, take time before you act. Resist reacting and look at ways to slow the process.

3. Next determine what is important and what you need to do to

take massive action in the direction of an important, non-urgent task. Rest first to gather energy and resources.

4. Next focus, plan and then seize the moment by acting. If you still feel distracted by urgent, unimportant and reactive behaviour, you can add the following steps:

5. Everyday affirm, "I anticipate, anticipate, anticipate now!" This gets your non-conscious mind expanding into what is possible and what you need to do to be a step ahead.

6. Switch off all of your push notifications on email and put your phone on silent. Choose 2 or 3 x 30 minute windows each day to check messages, and return phone calls. In between work on what is important, not urgent.

7. Reflect on modelling leaders who rest, plan, focus and then seize the moment and find ways to act in the same manner.

8. Appreciate that what you are experiencing is very common. I see it every day. Be gentle and kind to yourself and know that you can change and lighten your load.

Back to my business owner, he realised that much of what appeared to be a threat never eventuated into anything except wasting his time. He switched off email alerts and decided to read emails twice a day only. He gave himself just 30 minutes each time to do this. He resisted answering his phone continually and gave himself windows to call people during the day. Then he scheduled project time and activity goals to seize the moment. It took lots of discipline and self-control in the beginning, especially as he was overcoming the physical stress and exhaustion of being reactive all day. He now sleeps better and feels far more productive and confident.

To see procrastination from another angle may well have you telling yourself that anticipation is far more exciting and helpful for your business success. Know the feeling of being able to pace yourself, rest and then act. It's truly a refreshing relief to do this and you deserve it.

CHAPTER 25:
MONEY OR
MONEY & MENTOR?

"A mentor is someone who sees more talent and ability within you, than you see in yourself, and helps bring it out of you." ~ Bob Proctor

W hat's more important in business and leadership... money or the right advice? In this chapter, I share my experiences in relation to the choices around having finances and mentorship to assist you to create business success.

A friend of mine approached me one day and told me how excited she was that her brother wanted to support her sons aged in their early 20's by becoming business partners with them in a business project. The reasons for her excitement related to her brother's fine business skills which she thought would assist her sons immensely, plus her brother's wealth which she knew would assist the project in getting started.

No more than a fortnight later I saw her again and asked if the project had progressed. She told me it had progressed "after a fashion", but in a way that was not great for family relations yet great for her boys. Apparently, there were some challenges with the contract her brother had wanted to draft with the boys. His outcome was to document everyone's expectations, ensuring everything was properly documented. The boys were unhappy with the contract because they wanted to have the sole responsibility to sign cheques and make the decisions that would encumber the new company.

In my discussion, I learnt that one of the key objectives the brother had was to be available to mentor the boys and to assist them with the knowledge and skills he'd learned from 30 years in business. It seemed the boys valued their uncle's money more than his mentoring. The uncle wanted to help the boys so he gave them a choice. Money alone and he would give them an interest free loan to get started. In this offer, the uncle would have no involvement and no partnership in the business. Or option two, money and his mentorship as a business partner.

So what would you take, the money or the money and the mentoring?

This question takes me back to the old story about giving a man a fish or giving him the skills to fish for himself. Or the proverb about the two sons, one who chose a lump sum inheritance and the other who chose $1 that doubled every day.

A mentor is someone who has more experience, knowledge or expertise in a field and is willing to help a less experienced or less knowledgeable person. The gift in mentoring, as every leader knows, is that mentors can literally place a mentoree on the express train to success. They highlight and help the person they mentor to avoid all the learning experiences and pitfalls they went through to create their successes. A mentor also brings out the best in the person they mentor by highlighting aspects of their personality, strategies, communications and approach which are designed to create even faster and better results. Mentoring can save money and expedite rewards. The most successful business leaders in the world rely on the knowledge of people who have walked the path they wish to accomplish. Modelling happens in business and leadership when you follow a step by step system and I like to put mentoring and modelling together. The best mentoring will involve learning step by step systems that have been used by someone with the success you are looking for.

Mentoring is very different to coaching and in my experience many business leaders and entrepreneurs have chosen coaching at times when what they wanted is a mentor. A coach is someone who instructs, trains and creates a strategy, but, they may have never done what they are instructing you to do. Where I typically see this becoming a problem in business and leadership is that without direct experience of having walked the path a coach can fall short of the nuances that make a big difference in business. A coach who has walked the path is of course a mentor too, and this should always be investigated.

How can you find the best mentoring for your success?

1. Find a mentor who has the experience and expertise you are looking for and arrange regular mentoring sessions with them.

2. Join a networking group in your industry.

3. Follow successful business leaders in your industry and who inspire you on social media.

4. Read business books written by business leaders who inspire you.

5. Look at on-line courses and training by business leaders who have achieved great success.

6. Have a group of trusted colleagues and successful friends who you want to learn from and choose to spend time with

them.

7. Attend weekend seminars and courses showcasing successful business people.

There are a number of ways to find and gain immense assistance from mentors and successful business people in your field who you would like to model.

Getting back to my friend, her sons took the money. The brother apparently realised the boys valued his money more than mentoring so he called them and said, "Would you like to be mentored and have me put cash into this business or would you like me to put $80,000 into your bank account as an interest free loan and not join you?" They said they would think about it and call him back. The next day, instead of a phone call they apparently emailed him the account details. He promptly kept his end of the bargain.

It happens that I know the parties in this situation well enough to know that to be mentored by this businessman would be seriously valuable for any 20 year old. This is not about a judgement on money over mentoring. The boys in this case may very well progress to be incredible business people and this could be the wisest decision they've ever made. It's a choice. What would you choose? Why?

CHAPTER 26:
THE CURRENCY FOR YOUR EXPERTISE IS MONEY

"With limited money you can survive, with more money you can live." ~ Amit Kalantri

To learn feels right as a lifetime journey for me, so I attend many courses every year. I love to hear great storytellers and learn new skills. Often I meet new people and sometimes I see familiar faces at the programs I attend.

One day when I was attending a professional development course I was third party to a really interesting conversation between 2 people who had both completed a coaching diploma in Melbourne the year prior. It was now 8 months since they'd both qualified and the question hot on their lips was, "have you had your first paying client yet?"

The fact both were still yet to transact was the most interesting part of the conversation to me. What I was interested in finding out from this chit chat was why neither of them had been able to transact and earn an income after they had finished their qualification. This conversation reminded me of how many professionals I meet every day who do courses advancing their skills and personal development only to go back to work without advancing their leadership or pay.

The skilled professionals I was listening to both had a sympathetic response to the realisation and were almost relieved to know they were not alone. I knew what the course must have cost. They both have intentions to stop doing menial casual work outside of their field and immerse themselves into being in business. I realised they needed resources and fast, so I asked them a question:

"What is your currency for your expertise?"

Their answers were incredibly revealing. What I realised is that until both of these professionals feel within themselves that they are an "expert" who is appreciated, they will not be able to charge anyone for their expertise. Until then, their currency is not money.

An expert is someone who is very knowledgeable or skilled in a particular area. Money is a medium of exchange in the form of banknotes and currency that is used as a measure of value.

In western society, I find people spending money on upskilling and training without capitalising on their investment by increasing their income proportionate to the new skills they are employing in their work. This happens in all industries, and results in either a lack of career advancement or the start-up business that never gets off the ground. Why someone needs to transact in money relates to how they can afford to live a lifestyle which they decide makes them happy and gives them self-worth. You can do more good with money than without money. Money affords even more education and learning, health, lifestyle choices and personal freedoms. It moves people away from poverty, need and stress.

The history of confusion between appreciation as a currency and money as a currency often dates back to self-esteem and early programming adopted from parents, school, social and cultural groups. Virginia Satir (1916-1988) who was considered a trailblazer in family therapy wrote many books including, Your Many Faces: The First Step to being Loved in 1978. What Satir found was that many answers to the source of unproductive behavioural patterns could be easily recognised by meeting the rest of the family! When a person just wants to feel loved and worthy this becomes so powerful it overtakes their currency for transacting with other people. Often there is a matrix of beliefs holding this and other programs in place and the first step to clearing these beliefs is found in reviewing early programming by tapping into non-conscious thinking.

So if your currency is something that doesn't pay bills and you'd rather it was money, there are some steps you can take to move toward a shift in currency. This shift starts with recognising your early programming and the beliefs you might be holding onto surrounding your self-worth.

1. No matter how small the raise, every time you further your education and expertise look at how you can increase the value you give to your employer or clients. Take a step into the void by making sure even if in the smallest ways you are paid for this extra benefit. Even $1, if this is all it is, makes a statement about your intention to learn, translate knowledge into actions and be paid more as a result.

2. Look at the areas of your working life / career where you have increased your knowledge and skill without monetary reward. What are you gaining from this and if it's love and appreciation and this makes you truly happy then great! On the other hand, if you really feel that the investment of time and money in your education would be better rewarded in a

monetary sense, then open up to this option. Speak to a career or business advisor and get some assistance.

3. If you feel you have some limiting beliefs about your self-worth which may be preventing you from increasing your monetary rewards as you further educate yourself, then maybe look at finding a trusted colleague, coach or mentor whose abilities in the area are congruent with what you are seeking and ask them for some advice.

There's a chance you could try and fall short. If this happens, then professional career advice would be really worthwhile. Goal setting assistance and perhaps seeing a financial advisor would be a great idea. Above all be kind to yourself and realise this issue shows up in many people all the time. Appreciate that when you resolve this issue, if high on your agenda, you move toward what you want more of in your life.

Back to the question of, "Have you had a paying client yet?" I suggested to both professionals that what they fail to see in themselves is how the world responds to them. So we talked about their incredibly valuable talents and skills and the endless list of courses they had both invested and engaged in. This conversation opened them to possibilities and within a month both of them had made their first transaction with a paying client.

So what's your currency? If you feel like it's something uneconomic and you tell yourself you'd rather it was money, how does your life look when you move past this and have a currency you want in your business and career?

CHAPTER 27:
ATTITUDE

"Attitude is a little thing that makes a big difference." ~ Winston Churchill

The third time in one day was the moment I felt, okay universe, I'm listening. Have you ever heard a theme recurring in things said to you several times in one day and thought to yourself, "Hello, am I being given a message here?" I saw this happening one day and I share the experience with you in this chapter.

One day, I was making a presentation for a community group I am often asked to contribute to as a business leader. Today's event was a tiny lady celebrating a huge birthday. I was honoured to spend time with Lily King on the occasion of her 101st birthday. She has a smile that lights up the darkest room, is articulate and sharp, and is perhaps the most confident woman ever. She wore a pink streak in the fringe of her white hair and a delightful pair of brand new shoes to her celebration. Lily is living, truly living. At 101 years old she's out buying gorgeous new shoes. She made me think about life and the importance of attitude.

At this event, I learnt even more about the long walk to freedom that defines the late Nelson Mandela, how he stood taller and taller in his life and saw the seemingly insurmountable as just another reason to step up. I don't even know how that conversation started and it seemed to resonate with me at a very deep level. This conversation had me ask myself, "What personal attitudes did Mandela live by to survive and lead as he did?"

Later in the day, I heard from a 13 year old boy who was identifying with what he had learnt about himself and declaring that perhaps "boring" is not so boring after all. I was being shown the contrast of attitude for the third time in a day.

What is the message in all of this? It's just one word, the one word that has the ability to define every day of your life and change the world in which you live forever. Attitude. The definition of attitude is a state of mind or a feeling. In other words, attitude is the way a person views something and tends to behave towards it.

Why is attitude going to define your success in business and leadership?

An attitude of happiness, positivity, appreciation, progress, care and abundance is an asset in all areas of life. In career and business, your attitude has a massive impact on your ability to achieve your goals, to find happiness in the workplace and to be valued by your employer, colleagues and clients. In your relationship with family, friends and loved ones your attitude will define how people care for you and interact with you every day. In health, your attitude will enable you to reach your goals and have energy and vitality. Every area of your life benefits enormously from the quality of your attitude no matter what your life story or circumstances are.

The concept of attitude in psychology dates back to the early 1900's.

Thomas and Znanieki (1918-1920) studied the distinction between values and social attitudes. They found that attitudes were personality driven and shaped by subjective interpretation. In psychology in the 1970's theorists Bandler and Grinder found that pure experience has no meaning and an individual will make their own assessment based on individual values, beliefs, experiences, references and attitudes. Shrigley and Katz (1988) defined that attitudes are both verbal and non-verbal and have a significant impact on experience.

When I consider attitude and its importance in leadership and business I think of human transmitters. We use our energy to send messages and communication is only 7% words. Attitude is more than what we say. Your tone of voice, physical expressions and your thoughts can show your attitude. Have you ever walked into a room and felt you could cut the air with a knife? This happens because humans give off attitude and non-verbal messages without saying a word.

How are you going to take steps to ensure your attitude is your best asset?

Here are some steps:

1. Decide what your attitude is going to be in all areas of your life. You choose! A positive attitude helps set off endorphins in the body and these happy hormones help with stress management, mind clarity and general wellbeing.

2. Realise that attitude is not some Pollyanna (1913 Novel by E Porter) concept of illogical optimism and burying your head firmly in the sand like the proverb (Pliny the Elder from the Roman Era). It is real and you have complete control of your attitude. Life will still and always does happen. Events may be negative and you can still empower your thinking with a positive attitude.

3. Know that everyone sees and interprets things differently.

You can see the same event or movie and love it just as much as your companion hates it. Neither is right nor wrong. Everyone can make their own assessment and then share their beliefs. Whether you love or hate something you can still express and live with a positive attitude. Another person's attitude isn't for you to change. The only attitude you need to be aware of and manage is your own.

4. Attitude is a decision to bring out the best in yourself and others, to look for higher meaning in all situations and to look for opportunities to expand the boundaries of problems by finding new and better angles. This takes the courage to not take your life and everything in it personally and to define yourself by choosing your reactions, mood and perspectives. Choose to look for ways in which every experience can take you even closer to happiness and fulfilment of your life purpose.

In business and leadership your attitude acts like the positive and negative charge of a magnet. In mentoring many small business owners who are consultants relying on client bookings, the impact of a positive and negative attitude is profound. I've spoken to mentoring clients who are showing a negative attitude that is impacting their bookings and earnings and they have realised the problem and within hours of transforming their attitude from negative to positive have filled an empty schedule as if by magic.

What if you dwindle and start to feel sorry for yourself, and start looking for negatives, excuses and disempowering thought processes? Call a trusted friend and ask them for an attitude pep talk, write down the keywords on how you would prefer to feel and see how you could bring them back into your thinking, look for higher meanings. Go online and read stories about courage and a positive attitude from famous leaders. Model their approach.

Lily King celebrated 101 years of life and when I asked her what has kept her so vital and so energised for so many years the answer was obvious. She has an attitude of happiness, joy, certainty, self-love, ability and she radiates this every day and in all areas of her life. Mandela did not change his attitude despite conditions and persecution that would physically kill another man. Was it not for Mandela's attitude he would not have survived nor shaped history as he has done, creating a legacy that is like nothing we are likely to see again in our lifetime. A 13 year old boy negotiating the early stages of adulthood has realised that he has control of his mind and therefore his behaviour. This is all simple and powerful. Leadership and business success is transformed by the right attitude.

CHAPTER 28:
EMBRACING CHANGE

*"Your life does not get better by chance, it gets better by change." ~
Jim Rohn*

O ne day, I had an uneasy conversation with a staff member who was worried about change. Even though he realises he is safe, he fears change for no particular reason or at least no reason that he can articulate at this time.

This seems so common amongst many executives and what I commonly find is that the issue with change stems from an experience locked in the subconscious. This uneasiness is obsolete and no longer relevant. Fear, uncertainty and discomfort can be used as our compass toward growth.

In this chapter, I share with you the strategies I use to embrace change and look for the accomplishment in it. Change is an act or a process through which something becomes different.

Change can be helpful in many ways to steer us to an ever better life, help us find even more happiness, increase our confidence, have career progression, and move to places that are new and interesting. Everyone knows the stories of other people who have embraced seemingly impossible negative change and used this as a resolve to bring out the best in themselves and others. Pure experience has no meaning; the only meaning is the meaning we each give it. This meaning is determined by our values, life experience, rules, and the context amongst other factors.

In business and leadership, change is an important part of growth and achieving goals. It needs to be paced and happily embraced. Change saturation happens when too many aspects of a business are altered at the same time. Recognising this is also very important.

Brian Tracy says, "Develop an attitude of gratitude, and give thanks for everything that happens to you, knowing that every step forward is a step toward achieving something bigger and better than your current situation."

So how can we happily embrace change? Here are 7 easy, everyday strategies.

1. Look for a higher meaning in every change. Ask yourself what else could this mean? How could I see this in a way that will help me achieve what I really want? Sometimes the benefits of change are hidden until the space is made with the exit of the old.

2. Use a scheduler to "book in" all changes you need to make. For example, in one of my businesses we have a client with a significant back injury. She now needs to change her health status and take her care seriously. She has booked it into her schedule. For the next year, she has 52 appointments scheduled for treatment. What she has done is shown commitment for the change she needs to make in her life.

3. Ask a trusted friend to help you understand changes from another angle. Put them in charge of helping you find the "gold" in change you are concerned about. Make sure you choose someone who thinks positively and can help you progress.

4. Research how other people have dealt with the same change that you are faced with. The internet provides a great source of ideas. Recently, I had a client who was concerned about a restructure at work, and so he Googled the problem and found some great blogs and forums that completely opened the boundaries he had attached to the problem giving him great solutions.

5. Appreciate that how you respond to change is entirely your choice. There is no right or wrong. Take a kind approach to yourself. It's okay to be concerned, and the best way to combat this is to be the master of your mind.

6. When something isn't working in your life, leadership or business be open and actively seek change. I use an affirmation for this, "Universe show me the way to achieve the best results and change this situation now." There is only positive to be gained from inviting change in life circumstances that are not working.

7. Be aware of change saturation. This is the point where too many things are changing at the same time. The signs to look out for are subtle at first. I suggest writing a list of all change in progress and then prioritise them. Look at how each change is making you feel and if the answer is uncomfortable, write down what you want to feel instead. Then prioritise the changes in order of importance and in a way to benefit stability. Often there are some changes that can be delayed or helped with the engagement of trusted outside resources, a

friend or mentor.

My executive had his compass focussed on personal growth and when he aligned the changes happening around him as a part of the process toward even more of what he wanted in his life his ability to be in flow with the pace and rate of change increased. This assisted him to be significantly more adept at the process of managing change.

Change can be a new chapter toward living in alignment with the life you most want to achieve. If you've set goals for yourself sometimes considering that the changes occurring are a manifestation of where you are designing your life direction to go can make the process meaningful and perfectly guided.

"Change will not come if we wait for some other person, or if we wait for some other time. We are the ones we've been waiting for. We are the change that we seek."
Barak Obama

CHAPTER 29:
ACTIVITY TO CREATE A COMPELLING FUTURE

"What is worse than being blind? Having sight and no vision."
~ Helen Keller

Your DNA isn't your destiny. If you've decided you want to be a success in business and leadership and this quest has brought you to connect with me, one reason will always be that somewhere deep within you, the person you truly are knows that you are capable of everything you want in life.

In this chapter, I share with you how you can create a compelling future for yourself in business and leadership and why your family of origin and everything you've done in your life to date can have whatever relationship with your future you choose. Take all the good and leave everything else behind you.

I want to share a story with you. Three seemingly inconsequential personal decisions changed the course of a young woman's life forever. To know the true depth of how profoundly different life can be, you first need to know who this incredible woman was.

I meet many inspiring people and I recently spent time listening to a truly incredible life story and learnt much about how one woman created her compelling future. I met this woman on a flight and when I sat next to her I knew I wanted to talk to her. This is rare for me as I normally meditate and listen to music after a business trip. This was different. She is like an angel on earth and I felt this in her presence the moment I sat next to her. Born in jail to a young drug addicted mother she moved between institutions and foster homes from birth to the age of 16. In this time she was exposed to sadness, poverty and violence. At age 16 she ran away, deciding she was "old enough" to leave and lived on the streets and in boarding houses, mixing with the wrong crowd and earning a living through prostitution. She survived a violent knife attack and glassing in the face. At age 19 she had a breakdown. She describes it as the moment she finally asked herself, "Who am I, what's my story, what is my life purpose?" Now, more than 20 years later she is a remarkable gift to the world.

My question to her was how did she create a compelling future for herself, and more importantly make it a reality?

The incredible shift came when she made just three distinctions.

The first distinction was that she decided that life events are neither good nor bad, and so she didn't need to label them. She told me that everything in life just "is" and when she stopped beating herself up by labelling everything as either good or bad she became more peaceful and much happier. She used to label being born in jail as "bad" until she decided that it simply "was" and she did not need to give it a negative.

Secondly, she decided that she was resourceful. A youth worker volunteer she'd connected with spent what she describes as a good few years continually reinforcing to her that she was an incredibly streetwise and resourceful person. When this was reinforced enough, she decided one day to actually believe it to be true and to use this skill to make her life better.

Thirdly, she decided that she could trust herself, and part of this was making trustworthy decisions and not cheating on herself. She started being trustworthy to herself in small everyday events and then expanded on this when she had the evidence.

How could you take these distinctions into leadership and business to bring about powerful transformation and live the life of your dreams?

I have some steps for you:

1. Reflect on your family of origin, your grandparents, parents and your childhood. What, if anything, are the experiences of your early life that you are carrying with you today? Are these relevant and serving your highest outcomes for success? If you find the life journey and beliefs of your family or origin do not serve you or if these are just a part of your past you would rather leave behind, then do so.

2. Practice becoming very aware of how you label events in the world and your life. This process is about self-observation. If you see something on the TV news and immediately want to label it as "bad" or "negative" stop for a moment and ask yourself, "How might I view this event if I relinquish all judgement?" View events in your life in the same way. If someone cuts you off in traffic and you immediately want to label it as "bad" then stop. What might be going on in that person's life today? Is it serving you to be disturbed in a negative manner because of their actions. Be neutral. Try this on, it's an amazing revelation.

3. Reflect on challenging times in your life and think about the

resources you used to assist you to determine how resource-ful you are in times of challenge. See if you have any repeating themes regarding the resources you use when you are in a position where you need to effect change. Write a list of the resources you have used in the past. How could you apply these to business and leadership now?

4. How much do you truly trust yourself? Write a list of all the things you trust about the behaviours and actions you have taken in your life to date. How have these actions shaped who you have become? How could you use these even more in your life?

You will be delighted to hear who this woman is today. She could be your neighbour or a person buying coffee at the local cafe just like you. This is what I love about the power of leadership and human capacity. She is now 35 years old and is a gift to humanity. The pathway was incredibly rough. Her scars will be with her for life as a reminder of the circumstances she was in as a child and troubled teen. The rest of her is a truly remarkable example of the power of mind to overcome the dread, fear and sadness of a life labelled "bad" and make it something worth living for.

In my thinking, the resources she used to create a compelling future seem so distant from what one might imagine was needed. I am sure the three decisions she told me about were just a starting point. What is truly remarkable is the power of the human mind to make decisions and to step up to a higher level or meaning, trust, discipline and success. This amazing woman created this from a depth that I cannot fathom, and yet, for each one of us to apply her distinctions is an internal self-made choice.

She lives in Brisbane Australia and has created an incredible vision for her life. She went to TAFE to finish year 12, and went on to study social work. Today, she mentors young women who like her late mother are mixed up in drugs, crime and motherhood. In her own life, she is now happily married, has two children who she describes as her best creations and lives in a leafy suburb. She could be anyone, she knows she's someone and she has decided to be a leader.

CHAPTER 30:
SEIZING THE OPPORTUNITY

"To change one's life: Start immediately. Do it flamboyantly. No exceptions." ~ William James

In business and leadership, one key to growth and success is to identify and seize opportunities. In this chapter, I share with you how I do this and the steps to move forward by knowing when to seize an opportunity and then, how to identify whether you have made a good decision, if you need to make some adjustments or abandon it altogether.

Here's an old story whose origin is unknown. It's about a man who goes to a farmer and asks if he can marry his daughter. The farmer makes his request conditional to the man completing a challenge. He tells the young man that he will release 3 bulls one at a time into the yard, and if the man can catch one of them he will allow him to marry his daughter. The young man sees the first bull and it's so fierce he decides to wait for the second. The second is even more terrifying so he waits for the third. The third is meek and mild, he thinks to himself, awesome this is the bull I will catch. He positions himself ready to catch the bull by jumping on top and grabbing it by the tail, but, misses. The bull has no tail.

Are you waiting for the next opportunity, having not seized others in the past?

I was speaking with a colleague of mine one day while she was out and about in a shopping centre. It was hard to focus on the conversation with all of the external noise. Then she asked me to hold for a moment. Still listening in I waited and heard her ask someone for a Power Ball lottery ticket. When she came back to the call with me I immediately said to her that I was surprised to hear her buying lottery tickets. She told me that she was meeting God half way. I was very interested in her thought process. She said you cannot win if you don't buy a ticket. She told me she was seizing an opportunity because it is aligned with her wish to be wealthy.

How true is this in business and leadership? Opportunities present themselves all the time and knowing which ones to pursue is an important part of setting yourself up for success.

The challenge will always be how to choose the opportunities that are best aligned with your goals. Over the years, I have developed my own opportunity assessment test that I use to decide if I should pursue something, and then I refine as I go forward.

Here are the steps:

1. Upon hearing about a new opportunity, I always "check-in" with my intuition to see how thinking about the opportunity feels in my body. If you stop, close your eyes and take a few long breaths you will get a feeling. It may be nothing and I call this neutral. It may be unsettling and I call this negative and it may be positive, goosebumps or make you want to smile and I

call this positive.

2. Ask yourself how does this opportunity align with my personal and business goals? Get a piece of paper and write a list on the positive and negatives of the opportunity in terms of how they relate to your goals.

3. Next go back to the opportunity and ask yourself the following:

- Why should I do this? And why not? How does it help me achieve my goals or will it take me off purpose?

- What are the facts about the opportunity? Remember to separate from emotion. You just want facts.

- How would I undertake or get involved in this opportunity? What are the steps?

- What is my action plan if it's not quite right when I get started? What, if anything, am I skeptical about and how will I deal with this?

4. After you have completed steps 1-3 you'll have a good idea if it's worth pursuing or not.

If you do pursue an opportunity and it isn't quite as planned you need to act thoughtfully and consistently to be able to either keep it aligned to your goals or abandon it altogether.

Correcting a trajectory when you've taken on a new opportunity will take honesty, strength and self-awareness. There's little to gain by people pleasing when something is misaligned and going in the wrong direction. Speak up early, take responsibility and use "I" language. When you use "I" language you start statements with "I am" or "I feel" or "I need" and this means you are being accountable for your responsibilities instead of projecting and blaming another person. I think of corrections like steering a car. You are always moving forward in the direction of your destination and at the same time you need to keep your hands firmly on the steering wheel and move it to realign the direction as the road bends and the conditions change.

Knowing when to completely abandon an opportunity is essential. In my more than two decades as an entrepreneur I have had to do this many times. I see it as a normal part of being in business, leadership and acting with integrity as an entrepreneur. I have many stunning moments of this including an executive meeting once where a project costing tens of millions of dollars was abandoned by consensus after millions had already been spent. One person at the table who isn't a religious man by any account called it our "come to Jesus moment." It was a great decision and one that took an immense amount of self-examination and courage to make. Interestingly, the steps taken to come to this conclusion involved reading the signs that I have always used to know when to abandon an incongruent project or opportunity.

These are the signs I look out for:

1. Is this energising me or draining me? If it feels draining I will either review or abandon the opportunity.

2. Am I keeping my end of the bargain? Have I done the work? Am I being responsible and accountable? If the answer is yes, then I will reassess the commitment and the opportunity. If the answer is no, then I will act upon what I need to do with one important provision: If I continue to avoid the project and opportunity I have committed to then I see this as a sign of misalignment that means I need to reassess or abandon.

3. If I am working with others are they keeping their end of the bargain? Are they being responsible and accountable? If yes, then I will investigate why it isn't moving forward in the right way, and if no, I will ask them to help me to understand what's

happening for them in regard to the action steps needed. Based on this result, I will decide if the delays or issues are repairable or not.

4. Have I expressed my concerns to someone who can do something about it? If yes, what was the response? How satisfied am I with this response? If it feels that I have not been heard or the response does not help me to feel confident then I will either review or abandon.

5. Is this project being held up by the effects of universal intelligence? I tune into this as I see hold ups that cannot be sourced to a particular origin as a sign from universal intelligence that a project or opportunity needs to be delayed, changed or abandoned. If I get goosebumps when I ask this question I absolutely pause. This happened to me once on a very important marketing project that just kept meeting obstacle after delay after problem! I decided to just give it some space and within weeks a new government legal regulation was announced that meant had the project proceeded at great cost, the entire content of the marketing would have needed to be recalled as it was non-compliant with the new rulings. Thank you universe!

Moving toward goals takes consistent effort and when momentum happens it's because of individual effort. Secondly, you need to grab the big mean bull by the horns. Don't wait until someday. If you want to be a success in creating the life and business of your dreams, if opportunity knocks grab it. Don't wait for the next one. Leadership in business is about flowing with opportunities, knowing when to realign or abandon. Remember, there is no failure only feedback.

Follow an assessment system and keep it simple. Business success is about duplication not complication.

In our lives, we all have opportunities presented to us. The challenge is do we seize the moment and make life changes or do we let them pass and wait for our next big chance? In today's business world, seizing opportunities and making adjustments to steer the way to an outcome is a key to success.

CHAPTER 31:
WHO DO YOU NEED TO BE?

"The privilege of a lifetime is to become who you really are." ~
C G Jung

A number of years ago, I decided to spend a few days thinking about the question, "Who do you need to be?" I share this with you because it's been an expansive journey that has led to some profound learning which I have found truly inspiring.

Nelson Mandela had been in the news as his health condition deteriorated and while I read the news reports I asked myself, "Who did Nelson Mandela need to be to become someone of such influence and insight?" His story is a profound journey and words that come to mind are: visionary, tenacious, loving, passionate, resourceful, intelligent, thought leader, brave, invincible.

Then I find some of his famous quotes:

*"Resentment is like drinking poison and then hoping
it will kill your enemies."*

*"Lead from the back - and let others believe they are
in front."*

*"There is no passion to be found playing small - in
settling for a life that is less than the one you are capable
of living."*

*"If you want to make peace with your enemy, you
have to work with your enemy. Then he becomes your
partner."*

*"After climbing a great hill, one only finds that there
are many more hills to climb."*

*"Man's goodness is a flame that can be hidden but
never extinguished."*

With these quotes in mind, asking the question, "Who did Nelson
Mandela need to be?" opens up a minefield of possibilities.

So let's bring this back to the context of our own lives and those of the
people in our sphere of influence, I ask, "Who do you need to be to live
the life of your dreams?" And if you know who you need to be, are you
willing to do what needs to be done to be the best version of you?

In my work, I meet many people who say to me, "I'll start my own
business or apply for that promotion when I have achieved..." and they
move forward to list the conditions that they attach to being ready. We
sit and discuss the conditions and soon learn that the circumstances that
thwart advancement to business ownership are far deeper than a list of
"have" items.

What I learn is that many people's list of "have" cannot be achieved until they switch two fundamental aspects of how they live day to day.

In my experience, people who live the life of their dreams first decide to "be" who they need to be to do this. When this path is clear and they appreciate that they need to "be" someone, the next step taken is to "do" what the person they want to "be" would do. With ease, they find they can "have" whatever they want and live the life of their dreams.

There are a number of models in coaching that show this process really well, and I suggest looking these up. Taking it to the next level, Simon Sinek articulates starting with why, and for me this is also closely linked to the coaching model that makes goal achievement seem counter-intuitive. Sinek presents his "why" principle incredibly well and I recommend referring to his leadership in this model.

If you are willing to try an easy experiment, this week give some thought as you see stories in the media or reflect on people who inspire or sadden you by asking: Who does this person need to be to do the things they do or have done; to achieve the outcome they have achieved? In stories of people who inspire, and stories of people who sadden you, asking these questions will give you a profound opening to deeper insights. My experience with this exercise created a deep sense of compassion for others. The beauty in this is the compassion for self that is available when you apply the same questions to yourself.

Leaders who inspire us choose to be the person it takes to do the activities that grant them the outcome they seek. This can be used as a force for good and a force for negative. So, who do you need to be, to do what you need to do, to live your dream life?

CHAPTER 32:
RESPONSIBILITY

"Everyone sees who I appear to be, but only a few know the real me.
You only see what I choose to show. There's so much behind my smile
you just don't know." ~ Unknown

Have you ever had a sense that your duty to protect others and take blame is high? Do you sometimes wait for the moment when you hear a negative story about something that has occurred out of a perceived level of lacking accountability? Is how you show up in the world you live in sometimes impacted by duty, blame and accountability?

In this chapter, I share my views on responsibility.

One day after I spoke at a conference on business development and communication, I was approached by one of the delegates. She approached me and as she started to speak she was fumbling over her words and in tears, she said to me, "When I first saw you and heard you speak, I felt so intimidated by your presence and thought to myself that I should avoid you. What I have come to learn today is that you are so like me and even though we look different and you have a presence that I don't have, you are normal and have the same responsibilities as me."

Responsibility is defined as the duty of having to deal with something or someone. I have always looked at responsibility as the ability to respond or in other words the skill, talent or proficiency to react favourably. Choosing how to respond is high in levels of accountability as a leader.

Taking responsibility and having the ability to act favourably is a choice. The benefits include a boost to your self-esteem, peer appreciation and trust. Responsibility can also lead to abundance and a sense of accomplishment while you avoid the challenges of dependency.

To be powerfully responsive I suggest the following steps:

1. Deliberately choose to align yourself with what is good for you, good for others and for a greater good. Know what you value and live your values.

2. Notice what is going on around you and how other people react. Ask the best version of yourself how you want to be remembered in the moment. Act from this place.

3. Find small ways to make a big difference. I use the principles of the Expect a Miracle project started by an Australian man John Hinwood. I carry cards with the words "Expect a Miracle" on them and hand them out randomly when I feel connected and want to make an even greater difference to someone's life.

4. Inspire others with your reactions. Allow people to see who you really are. Share your thinking with them and be prepared to be honest about the trials and tribulations that have led you to be the person you are today.

5. With events that trigger you negatively, unpack the meanings

you are putting on these events and see if there may be different ways you could respond. What outcome could you gain from the ability to respond differently?

6. Appreciate that all people have their own opinions and views, none of which are any of your responsibility or your business.

I would argue that the woman at the conference had an amazing presence and that her level of honesty and accountability for her judgments was inspirational. In speaking to her, she was able to gain insights into how she was also responsible for having a high level of integrity with how she presented herself to the world and that this would elicit different responses for everyone she encountered. The basic premise of our discussion was about the great leveller of responsibility and how it does not discern between perceived or imaginary rank or stature, class or life journey.

Responsibility is open to everyone as a decision for progress and finding higher meaning.

CHAPTER 33:
SUCCESS THROUGH OTHERS

"A leader is best when people barely know he exists, when his work is done, his aim fulfilled, they will say: we did it ourselves." ~ Lao Tzu

I n this chapter, I share with you one of the most loved pieces of advice in business I have ever received. I have remembered and used this every day for the last 25 years.

First, I want to share the story of its origin. In 1960, a young immigrant couple from Europe were married in Sydney. In these times, it was customary to ask a man who you looked up to and who you thought could lead and support you in times of need to be your Best Man. Unlike today, in the 1960's a Best Man was not your closest buddy who knew how best to ensure you were hammered on your bucks night and could articulate the worst of you in a wedding speech. He was often chosen because he was a mentor and someone older and wiser who could guide you.

At this wedding, more than fifty years ago the young couple were only slightly older than a school leaver and were both already working hard for a living, she in a bank as a secretary and he as a chef. The Best Man stood up to make his speech and he offered the couple the best wedding gift he could think of.

He said to them, "I have bought you a gift, a material possession of crystal and gold to commemorate this day. It is worthless in comparison with the best gift I can give you and this gift is my advice... If you want to be successful beyond your wildest dreams, learn how to be effective at delegating."

I meet so many business leaders who are completely exhausted, battle weary and burnt out. In an effort to lead, they put themselves in an unrealistic depth of work commitment and stress.

Real leadership in both large and small business is success through others.

One key to success I have always lived by is to bring in the experts. I have a vision and skills and at the same time the efforts, expertise and involvement of others in the business projects I undertake are critical to my success. Today in one of my businesses, I am the only non-Chiropractor in Australia who owns a large and successful Chiropractic clinic. In my business, I have a team of experts in their field qualified Drs of Chiropractic and they are responsible for the work they are skilled at. I have an expert industry based practice manager and assistants who have experience and expertise in the health and wellbeing industry. What I bring to the business is leadership and communication mentoring, entrepreneurship, business systems and marketing expertise.

To be a leader who achieves enviable success in your work, and at the same time has life balance I suggest doing the following five things:

1. Deliberately find and work with people with more skill and knowledge than you.

2. State your goal clearly, and encourage individuals to demonstrate even better ways to achieve it.

3. Stand by the decisions of people in your team, and be accountable even if the decisions don't achieve the desired outcome. Empower suppliers, contractors and staff to feel they can always positively amend a mistake.

4. Live the motto, "leadership is success through others."

5. Create an environment that brings out the very best in people.

The couple who received this advice in 1960 are my parents. My late father, Theo Moulis, was an accomplished restaurateur in Australia who was a successful business owner running his fine dining establishments for more than 60 years. He arrived in Australia on a boat at age 16. He never completed school and although he could read his written English was poor at best. He owned multi-million dollar businesses employing the best staff he could find. He lived the motto of success through others.

Leadership does not need to drag you to the depths of working to the bone. It can be an energising and incredibly light filled experience. When leadership is success through others the aim is to find the very best people, with the very best skills. The key to success through others far outweighs the practical skills of you the leader.

TRANSFORM YOUR SUCCESS EVEN MORE

"A leader is one who knows the way, goes the way and shows the way."
~ John C. Maxwell

H aving a mentor by my side has been transformational in my life and I love to make a positive impact working with people just like you.

I would love you to join the vibration of Conscious Communication by visiting my website at www.madelainecohen.com and signing up for my FREE weekly Conscious Communication inspiration. You will hear from me every Monday morning with profound stories and ideas that you can use immediately to transform your own mindset, family, friends, colleagues and your community.

Mentoring

"When a leader lifts, everyone around them lifts too."

The work you do with me, has a ripple effect on everyone in your life. You will lead conscious communication within your family, relationships, businesses, and make an impact. Learning how you can make an impact rather than what you can get from a situation, will transform how you engage with the world.

In my working career I have delivered over $100M in sales to my clients and I thrive on helping people from what feels like a blank page. I have made a career of putting myself in situations that are seeming impossible – eg., like someone far removed from the boys sports club ending up in sports marketing negotiating multi-million dollar international deals; and a non-doctor owning one of the most successful healthcare practices in Australia.

All at the same time negotiating my way through 6 years of IVF to completing a complex divorce settlement in 3 months without a lawyer. We continue to work together and co-parent happy children who excel at school, music and sport.

The high road isn't easy, but at the same time it doesn't have to be a drama that feels like it is destroying your life. When you have the resources to make the complex into simple, you can get through it with grace and dignity.

I have walked the path before you, everything I share with you is possible, because I have done it!

How 1:1 Mentoring Works

- Your session starts with me from the moment you book, I will get a sense of you and determine the best strategy for our time together.

- I typically work with clients by phone and/or Skype, so you can be anywhere for these sessions; you could be in an airport lounge, in your car, out in the garden, in your living room. I don't want our mentoring to be an interruption in your life, I will fit each session around you.

- Sessions are for 1 hour, weekly or fortnightly, for 12 months. All sessions are recorded and I will send you this audio file at the end of each session.

- Payments are made by direct debit every month, so you don't need to spend the mental energy remembering to pay. Some of my clients have their sessions paid for by the company they work for.

These sessions can cover how to:

- Accelerate your career success

- Learn how to deal with drama

- Rise above workplace stress

- Learn what's behind the words people say

- Achieve holistic health outcomes

- Innovate and save time

- Become even more productive

- Create a life of balance

- Set and maintain healthy boundaries

- Take relationships to a higher level

- Find people who you resonate with

- Attract prosperity in your life

For more information and to complete an enquiry form go to www.madelainecohen.com or contact us on +61 2 9211 8153.

"Birds of a feather flock together. Energy is contagious. If you want to fly with the eagles, you'll have to stop swimming with the ducks."
~ from Secrets of the Millionaire Mind by T. Harv Eker

Contact Madelaine Cohen:

W: www.madelainecohen.com

E: madelaine@madelainecohen.com

P: + 61 2 9211 8153

L: www.linkedin.com/in/madelainecohen

ABOUT THE AUTHOR

Madelaine is a successful business leader and entrepreneur with a deep generosity in how she shares her most innovative communication strategies and "light bulb moment" experiences in leadership development, communications, marketing planning, commercialisation, sales, business and financial success. Her approach is entertaining and above all incredibly practical and life changing.

A businesswoman whose self-made success involves working with Government based organisations and some of the largest companies in the world she has 25 years of experience as an entrepreneur, accredited training leader, mindset expert, speaker and mentor. Her leadership capability is expansive and she delivers results for senior executives and helps business owners. After "retiring" at the age of 21 to be an entrepreneur Madelaine has inspiring stories of hard work, immense personal and professional challenges, opportunities and success. As a business mentor she gets right to the point and compresses years and sometimes decades of learning into a session to create an immediate breakthrough.

In the early-1990's, Madelaine started her first business as a consumer products marketer including consulting for 15 years to Olympic, Commonwealth and Asian Games Committees. In this time, Madelaine's team delivered profitable and innovative multi-million dollar marketing programs to major sporting event organising committees globally. At the same time, she consulted and became the owner of a clinic in the healthcare industry.

Madelaine is the owner of Chirofamily Chirosports a well-loved Chiropractic clinic in Sydney's Eastern Suburbs which has been established for more than 20 years. She is probably one of the only non-practitioner owners of a highly successful independent healthcare practice in the Chiropractic industry in Australia. Her success in diverse business interests is attributed to her mindset, leadership and marketing skills. She is intuitive, a lateral thinker and reverse engineers business opportunities with formidable success. As a business mentor, Madelaine's experience and expertise transforms draining to amazing with step by step solutions and immediate results. She is an entertaining keynote speaker and a marketing and brand expert who mentors business people in the service sector who want to truly excel in professional development, communication excellence, influence, wealth creation and leadership.